Hello to all my creative friends.

I hope you enjoy this Christian Coloring Book with Scripture as much as I loved creating it.

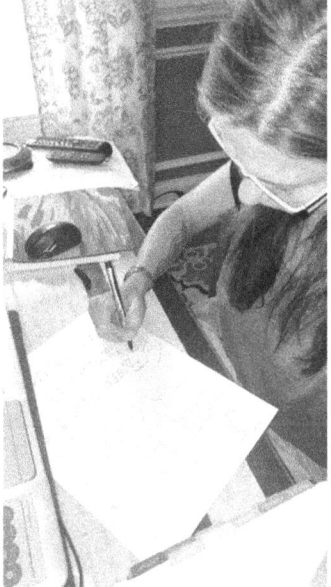

I should probably be embarrassed to admit this, but often, when I go art supply shopping, I find myself acting like a kid in a candy store. I want to try everything, I want to buy everything and I often put everything in my cart (and then have to return it before check out!). There's just never enough time to do it all and certainly never enough money to buy it all. But that's ok, because the fun is really in the actual trying different tools and techniques!

Prior to losing my job, I never allowed the artistic side of me to flourish. In fact, I'd draw and then hide it away. I refused to acknowledge my inner voice which was continually nagging me to keep going. One thing I have learned is that part of being an artist is appreciating the time to be still and allowing yourself to follow your intuition. I find that my artistic endeavors are intertwined with my spiritual journey. In my world, one does not exist without the other. There are enormous benefits to allowing your spirituality to enter into your time of creation. God is in all things and without His presence, creations tend to lack that shiny luster that makes them so desirable. I pray that you get to spend some real one on one time with God as you go through these pages. I ask Him to let you really experience, all that His presence in your creative time, has to offer!

As a self-taught artist, I am thrilled when someone enjoys my work enough to purchase it and put it in their home or business. I thank you for having the confidence in me to allow me to help you with your journey! The process itself is where I find my true joy. For me, it fills a void that I don't always realize is there! I feel that each one of us is drawn to certain events as we need them and mostly, as we are ready for them. For me, that time is now! This is my journey and I am beyond excited to share it with you!!!

Again, I am so grateful for your support and confidence in me! Please feel free to drop me a line at denyse0213@gmail.com and let me know how I am doing and how you feel about the works of art I have presented. I'd love to hear your stories!

Hugs!!!
   ~Denyse~

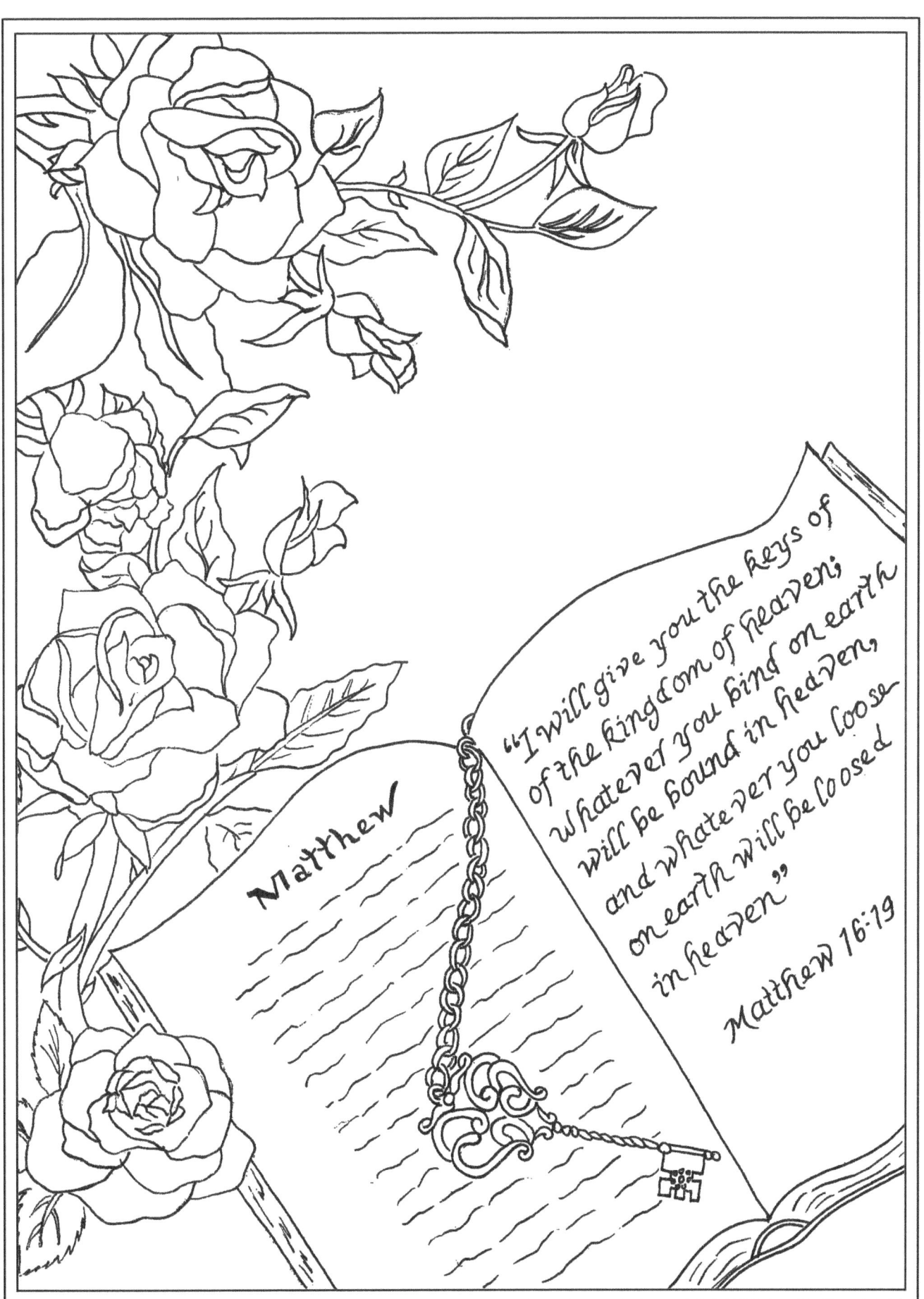

Matthew

"I will give you the keys of the kingdom of heaven; whatever you bind on earth will be bound in heaven, and whatever you loose on earth will be loosed in heaven."

Matthew 16:19

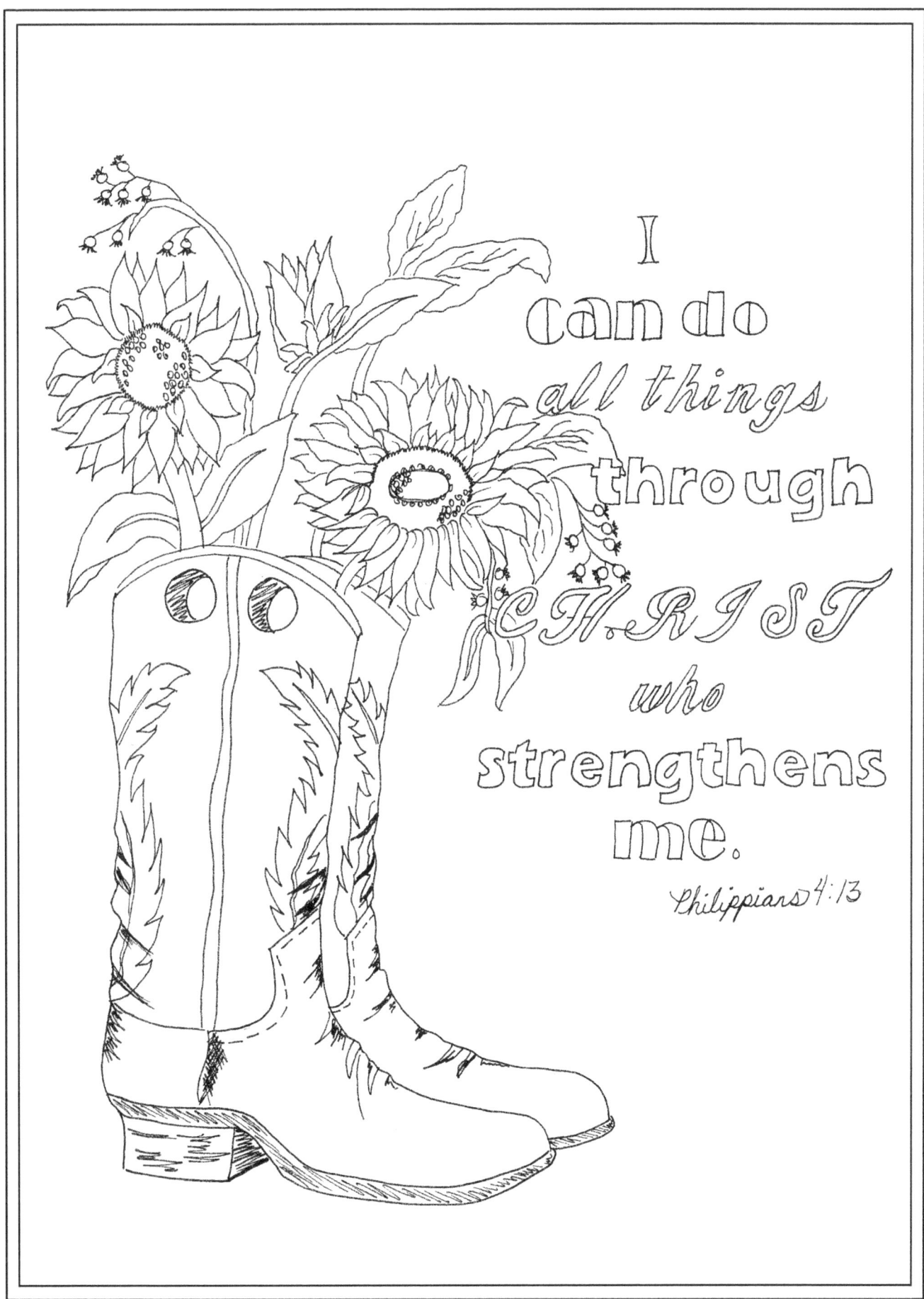

I can do *all things* through CHRIST who strengthens me.

Philippians 4:13

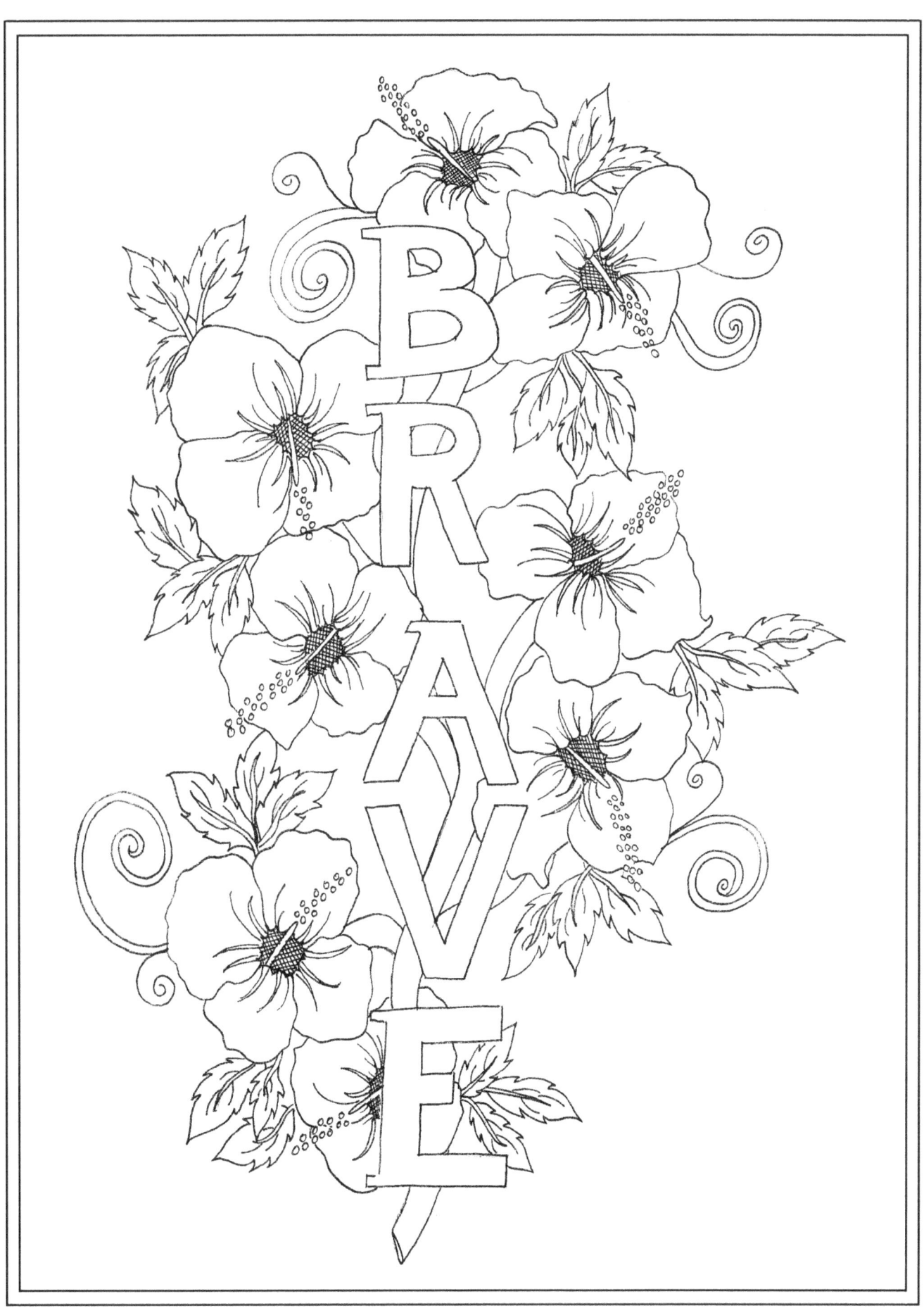

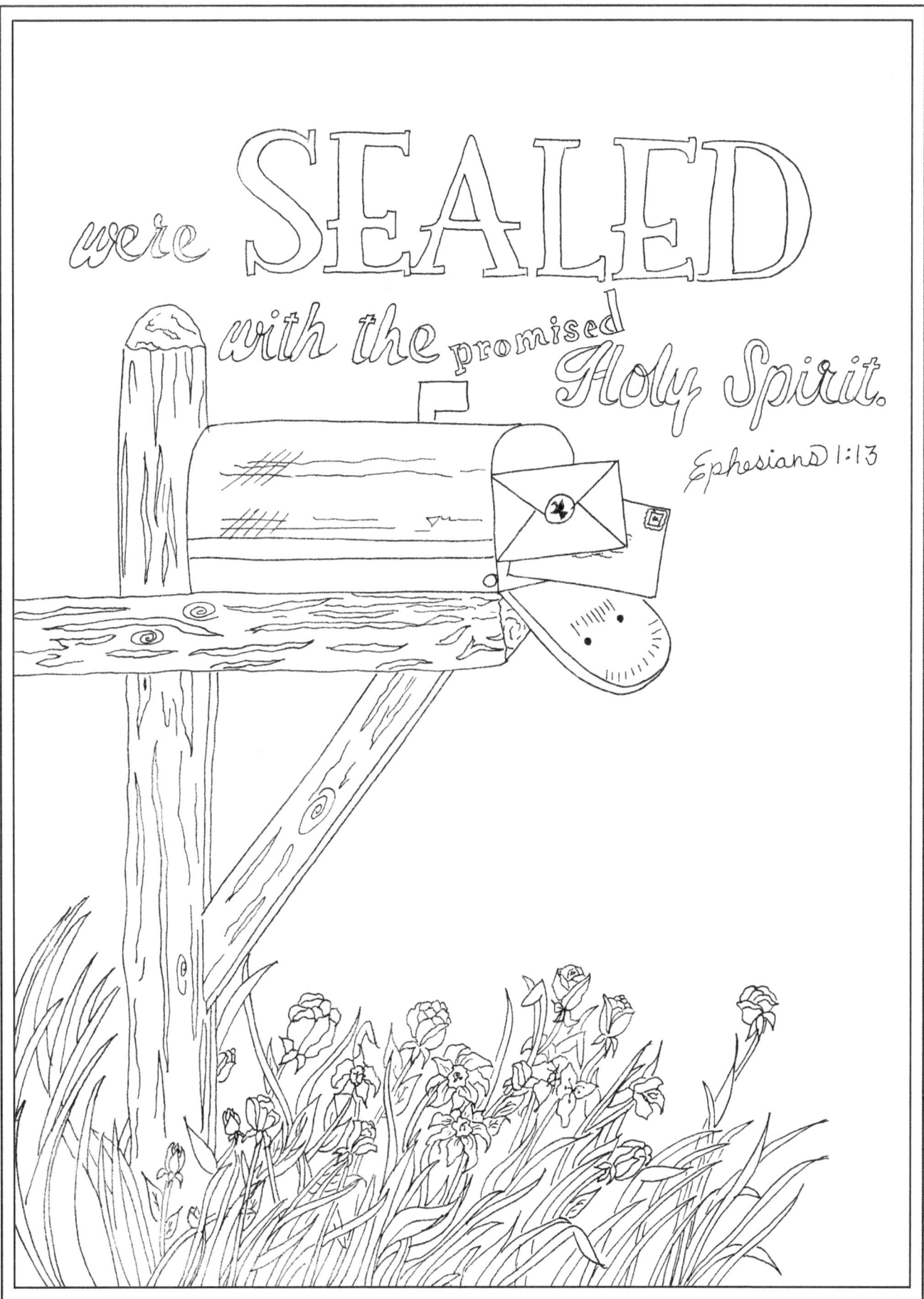

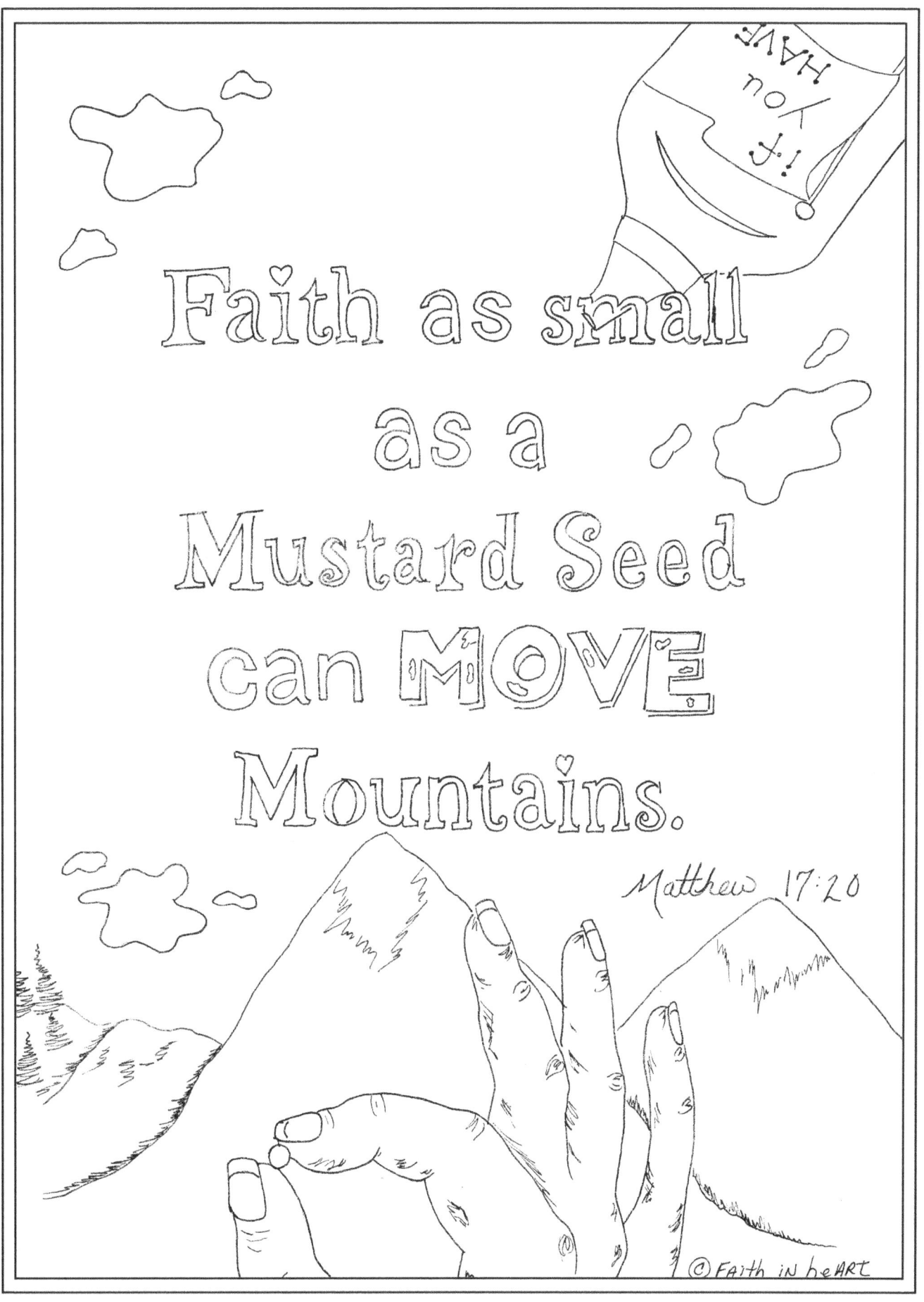

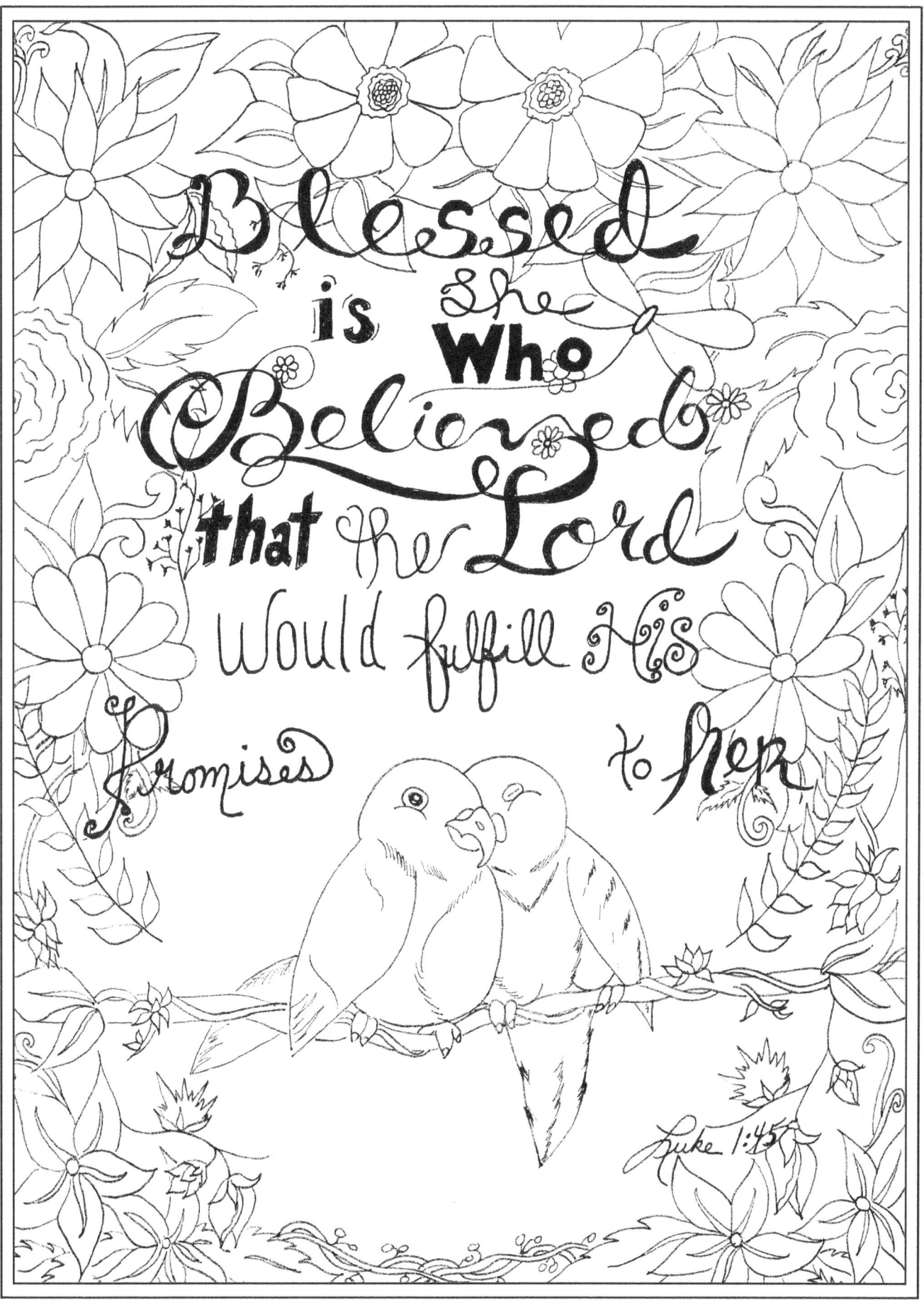

Blessed is she Who Believed that the Lord Would fulfill His Promises to her

Luke 1:45

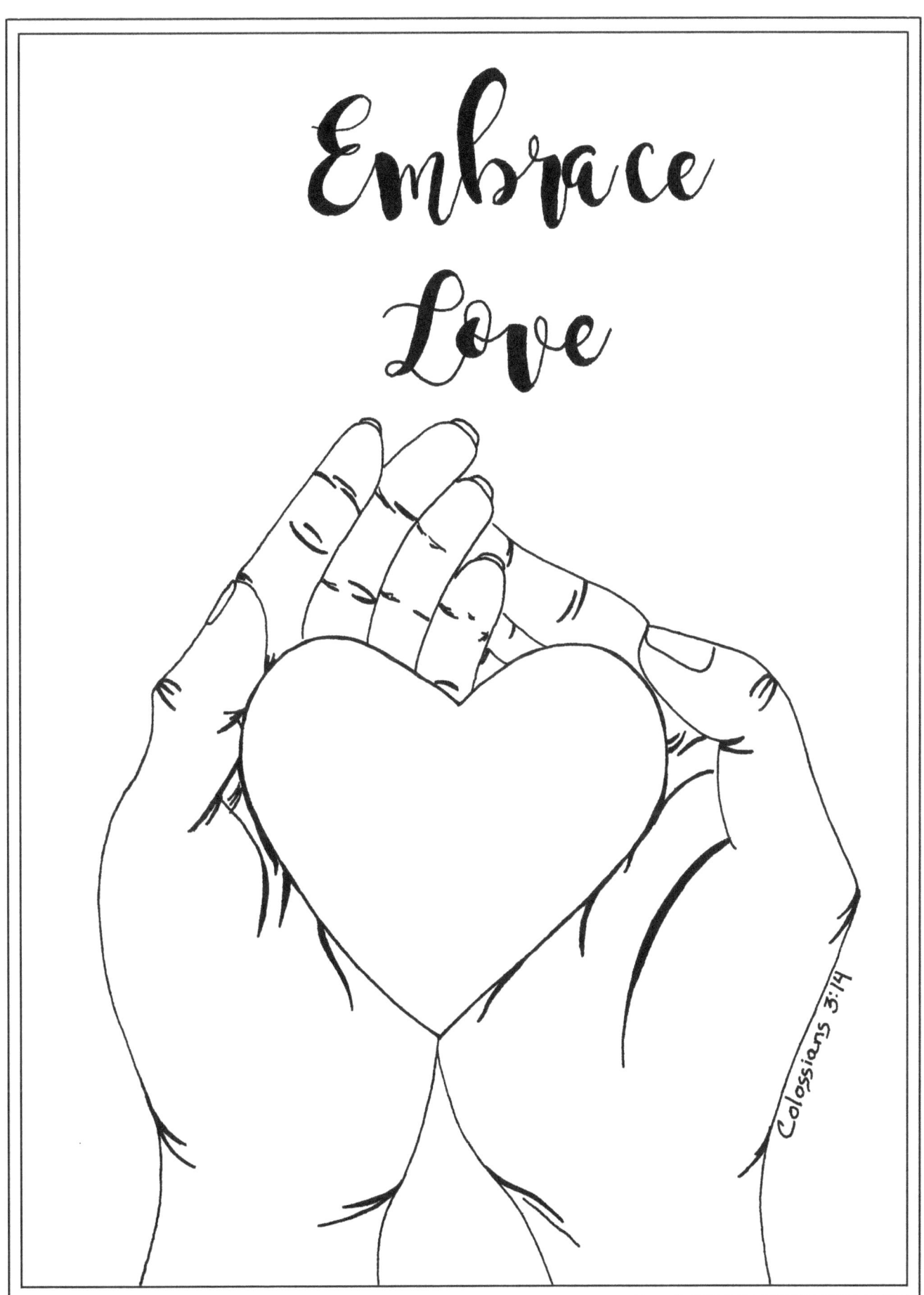

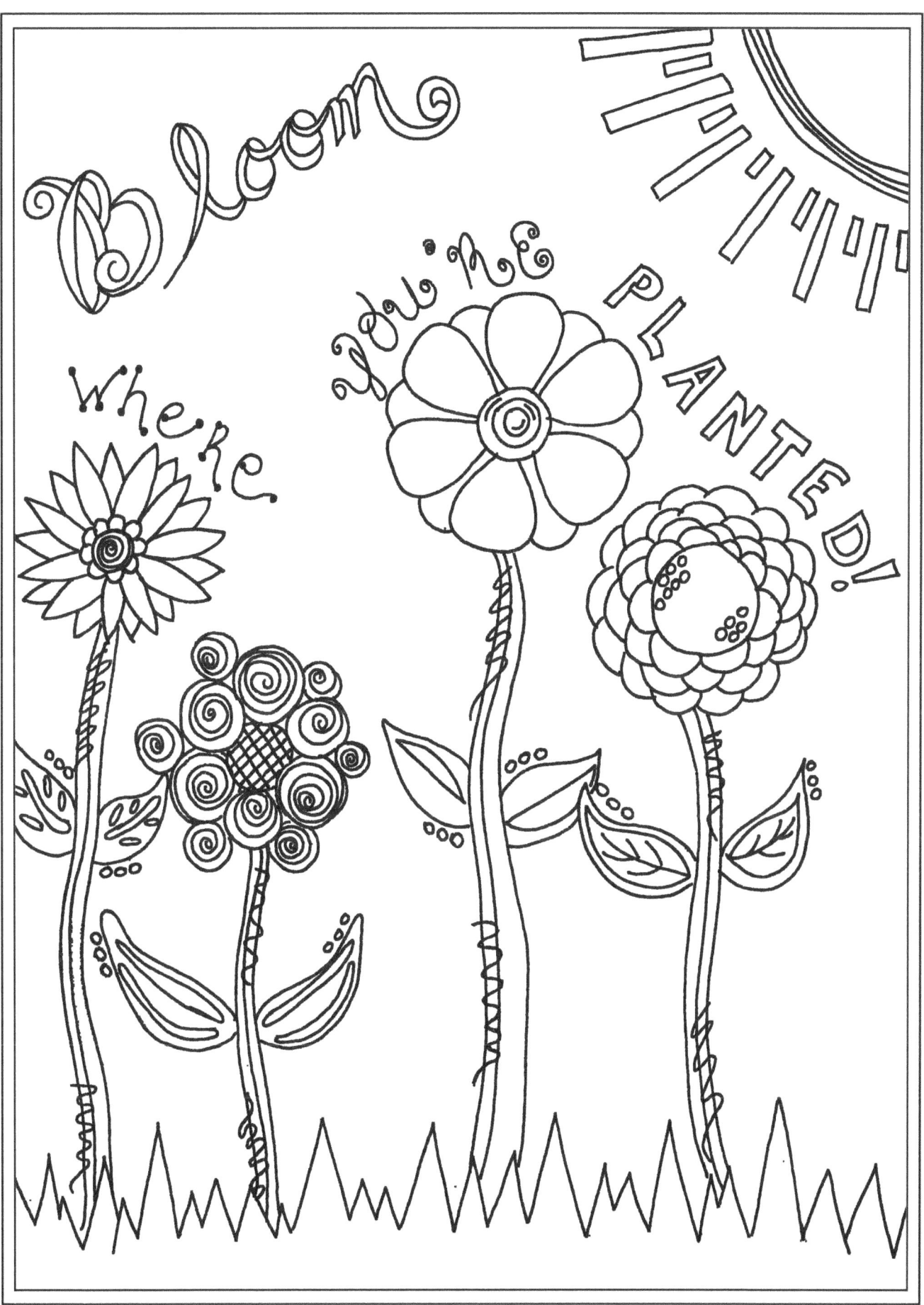

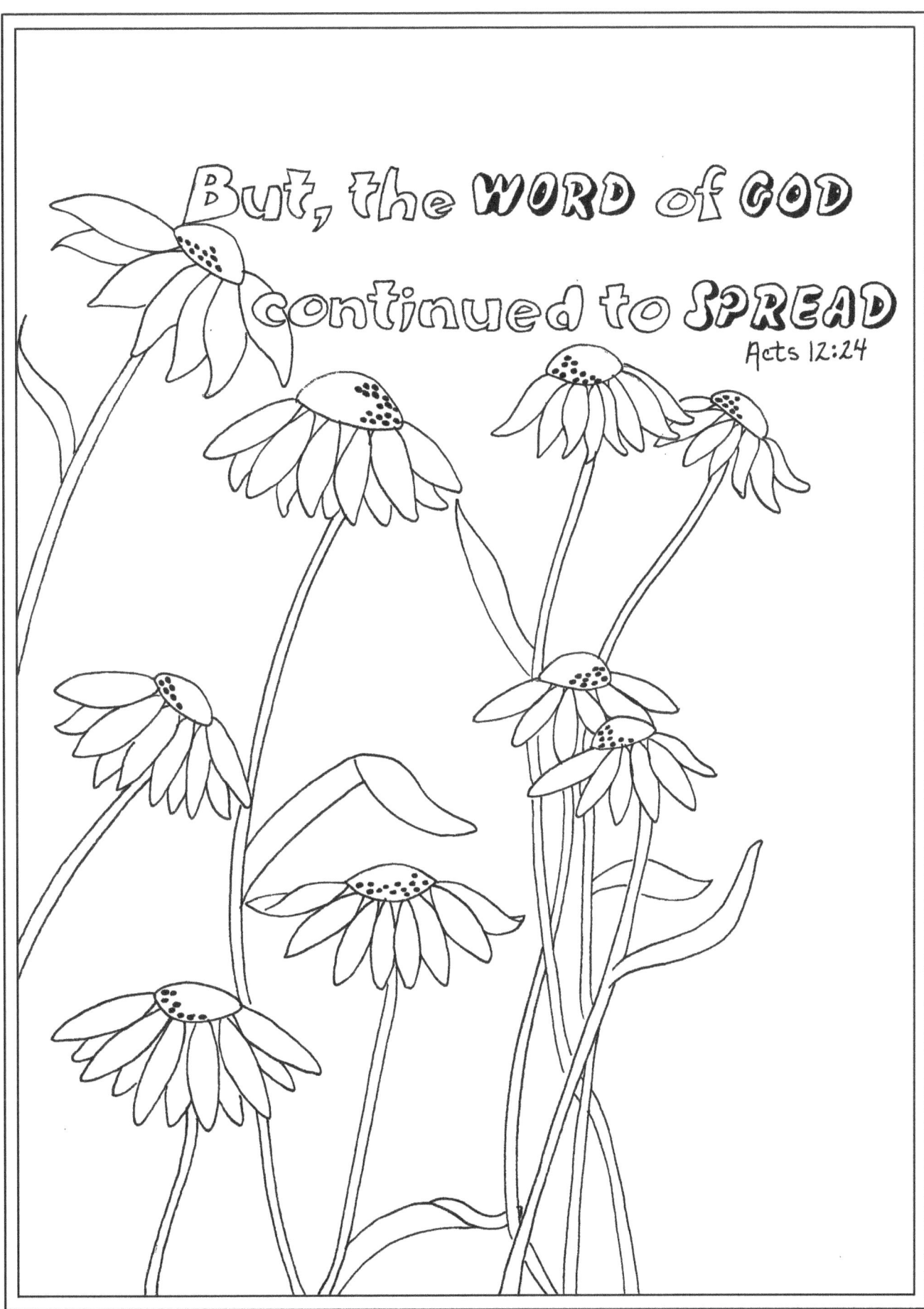

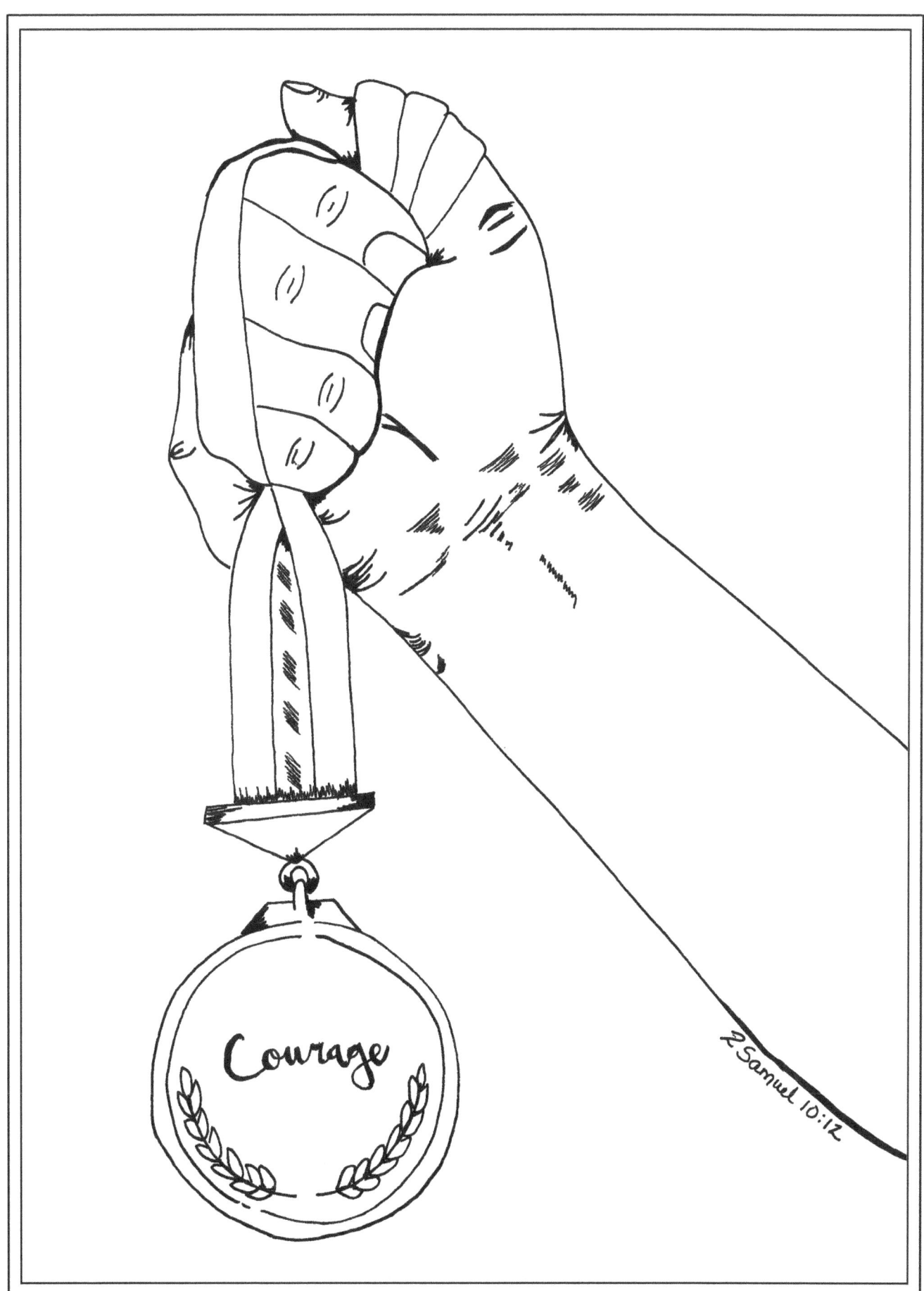

SPEAK TRUTH EVEN WHEN IT HURTS

— 1 Samuel 3:17

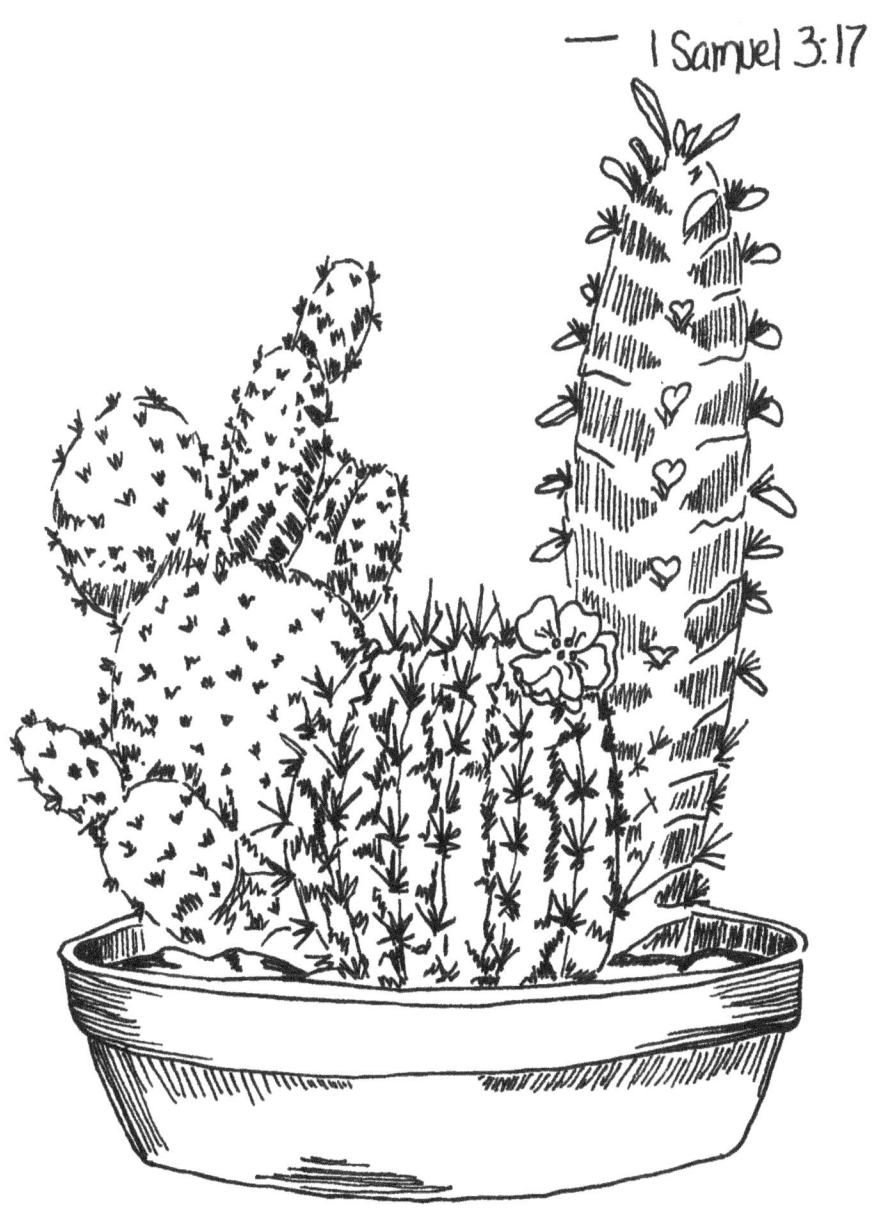

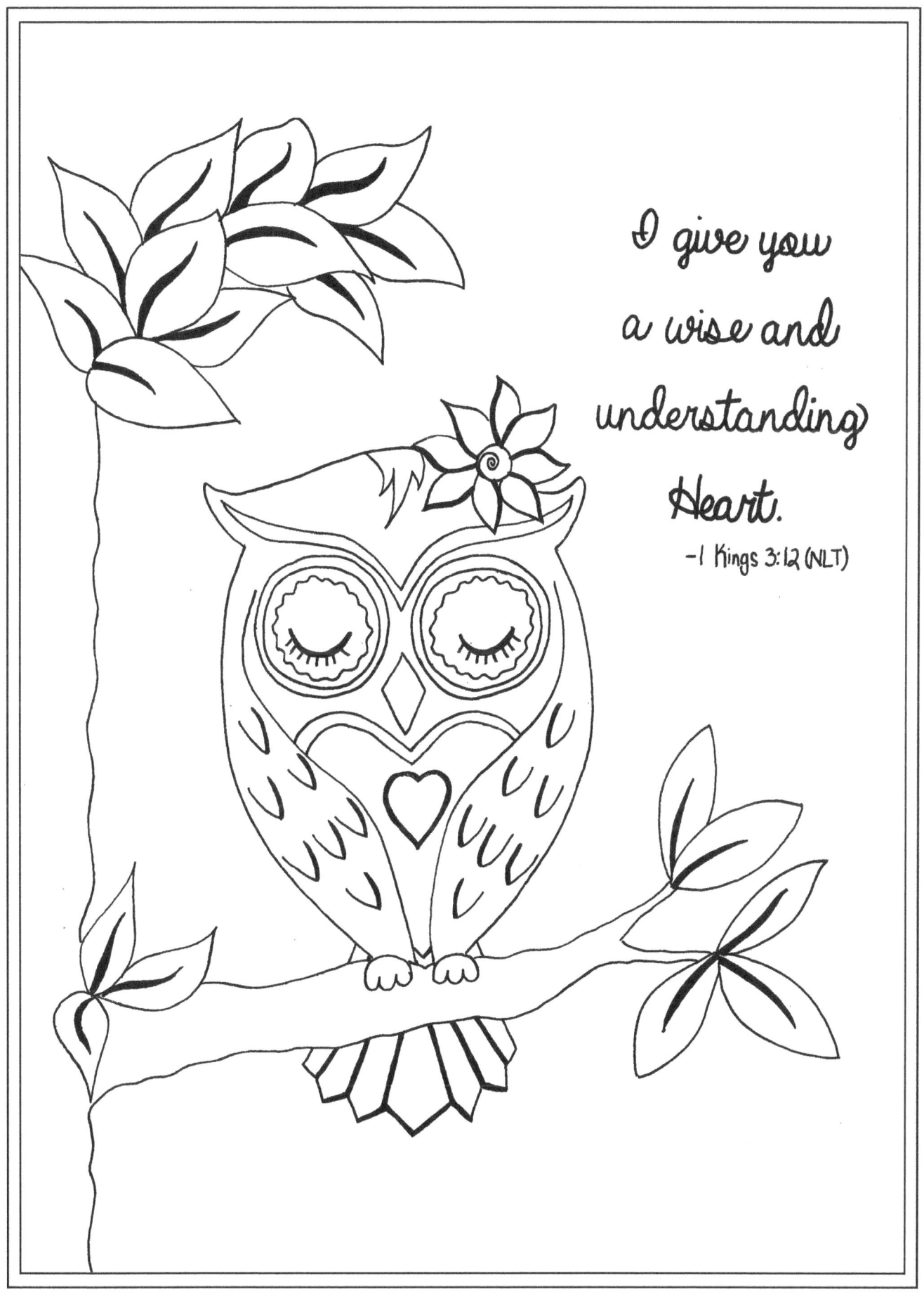

I give you
a wise and
understanding
Heart.
-1 Kings 3:12 (NLT)

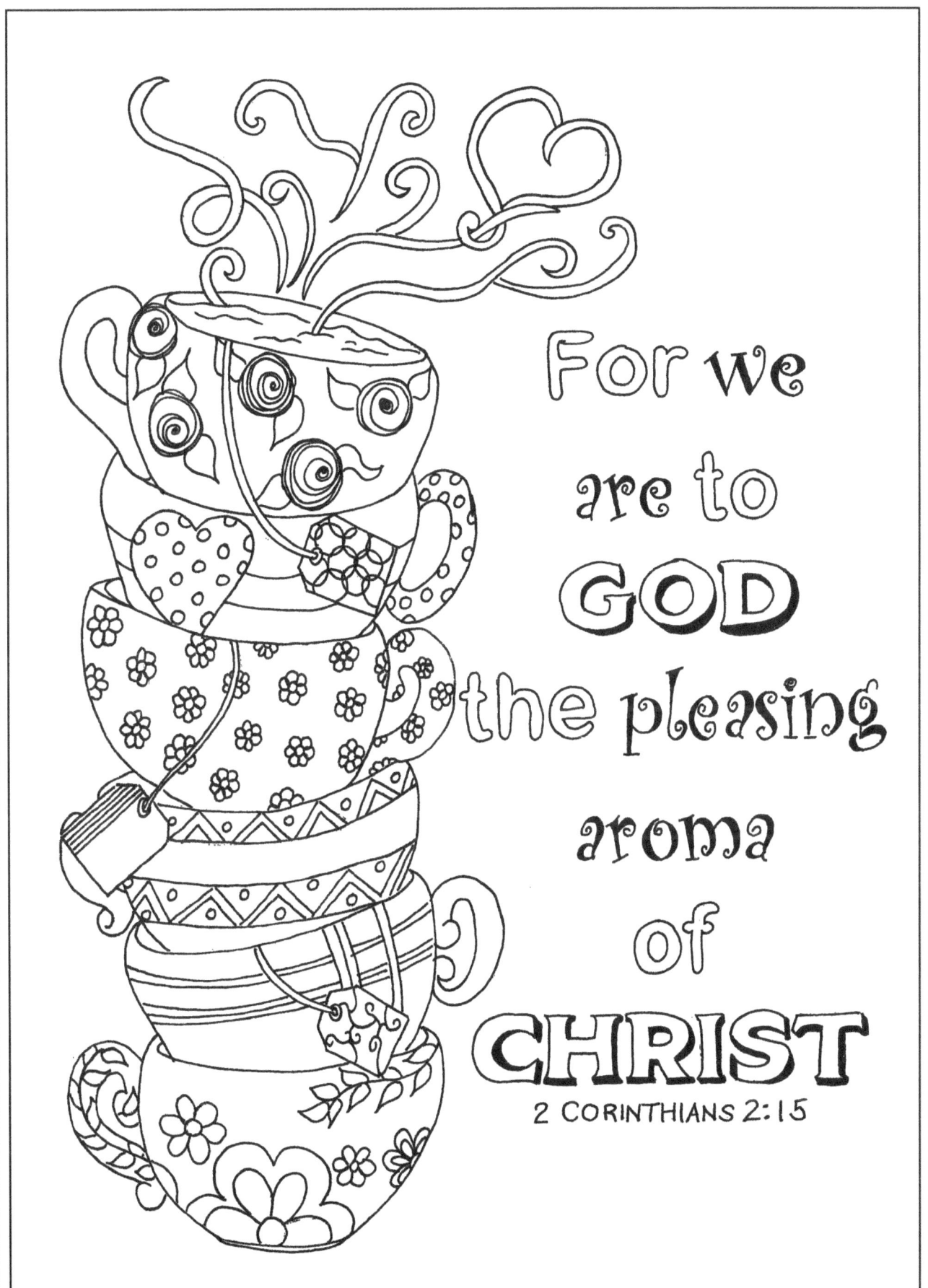

For we are to **GOD** the pleasing aroma of **CHRIST**

2 CORINTHIANS 2:15

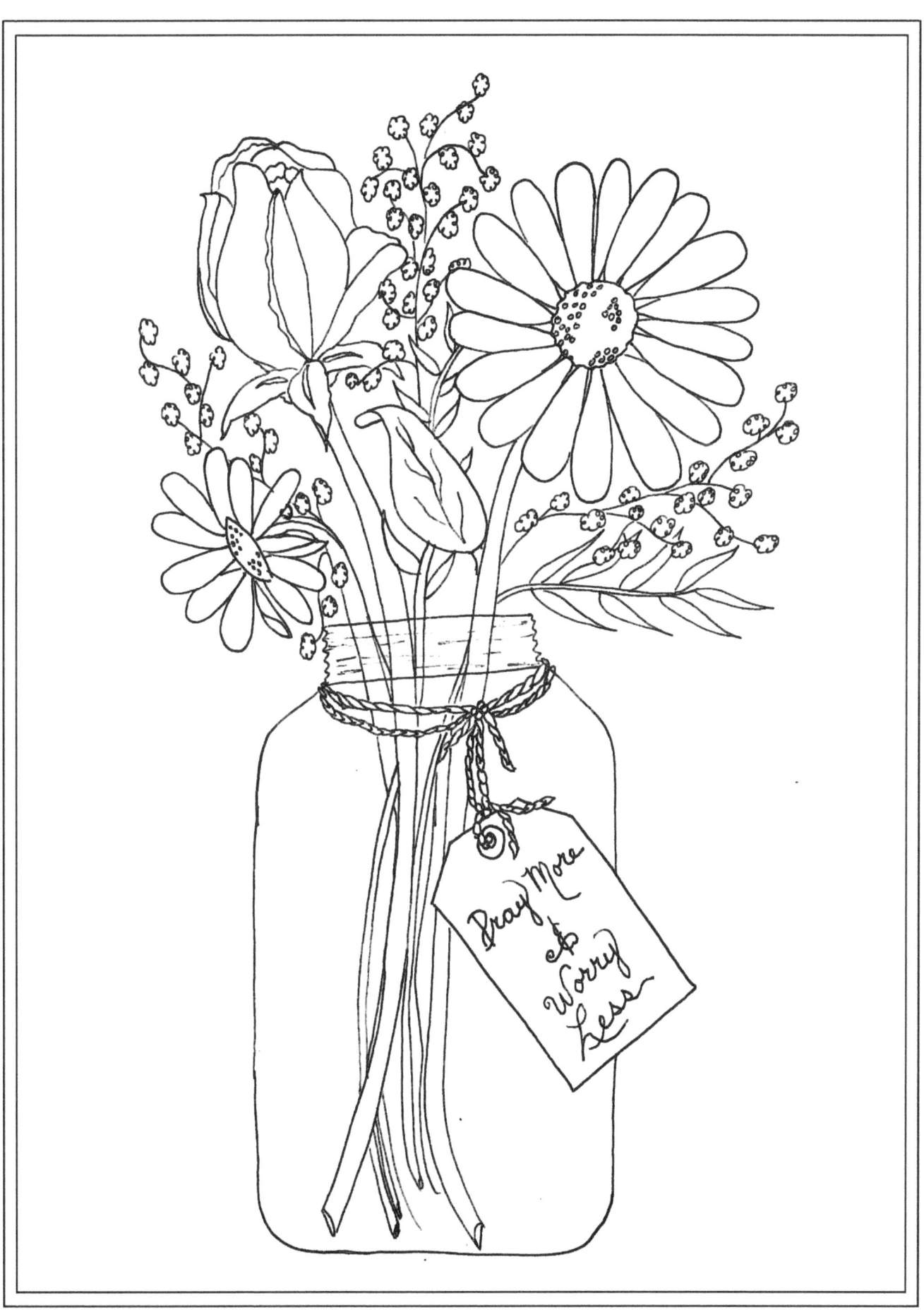

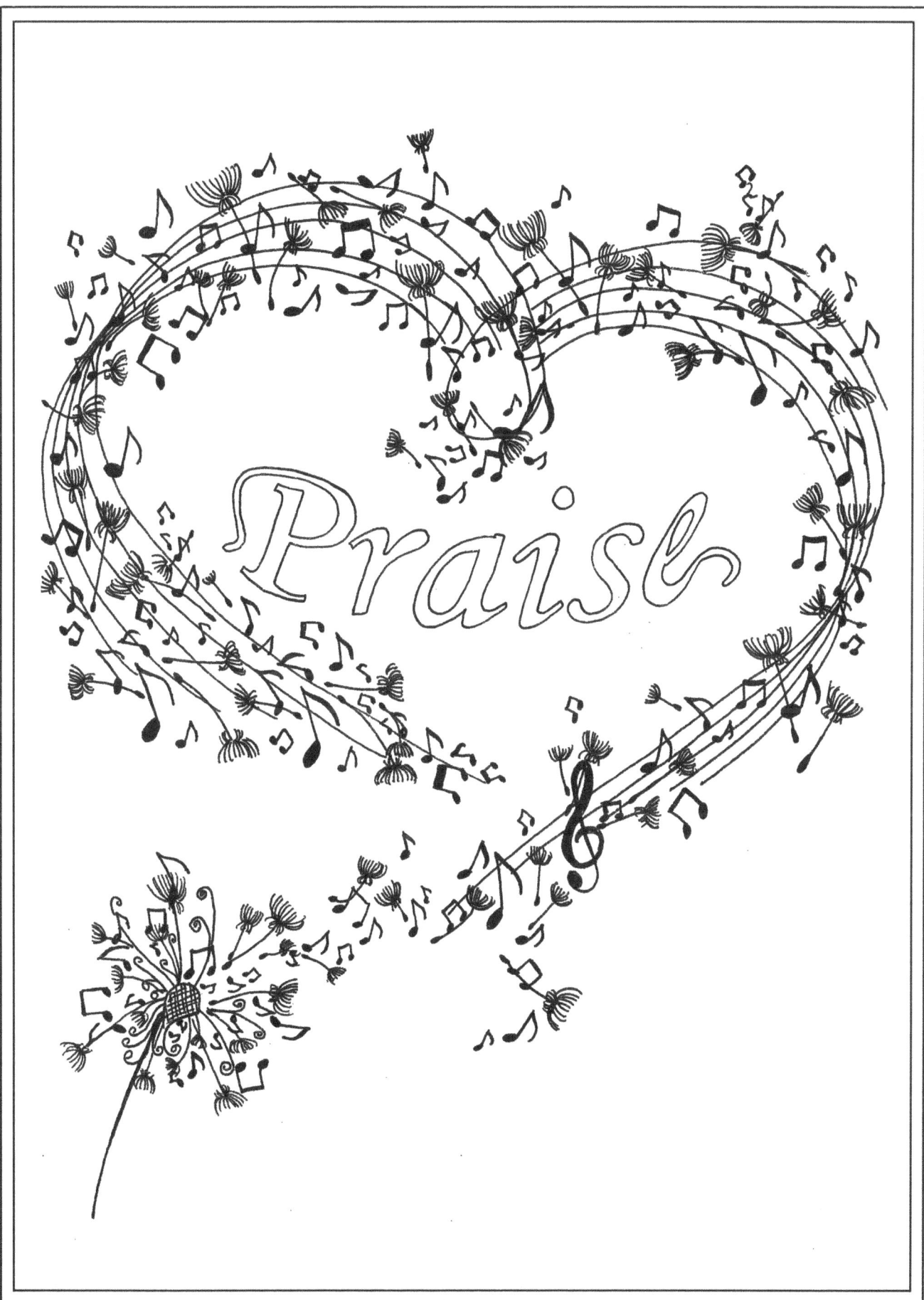

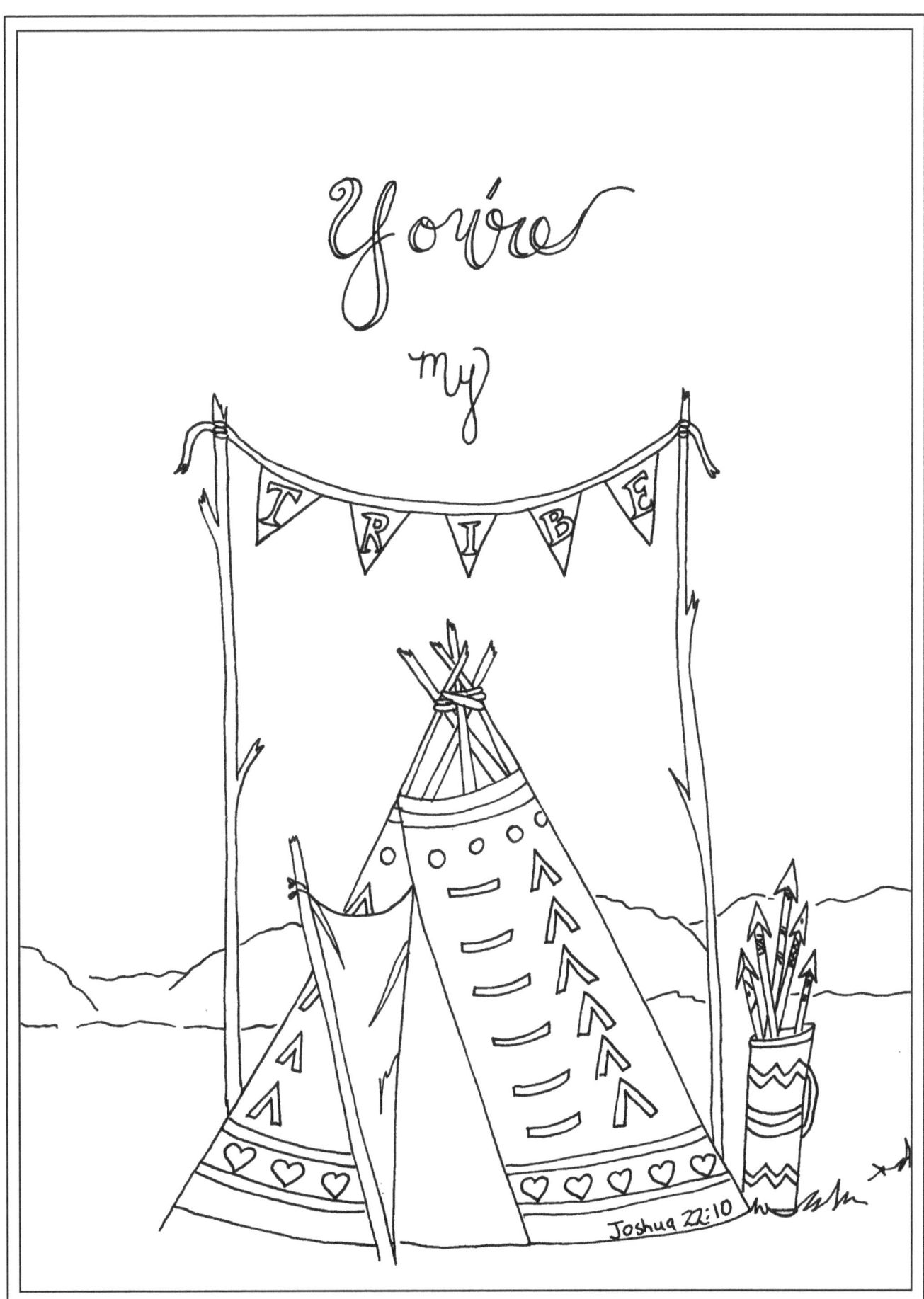

Seek THE LORD WHILE HE MAY BE found. Call ON HIM WHILE HE IS near.

Isaiah 55:6

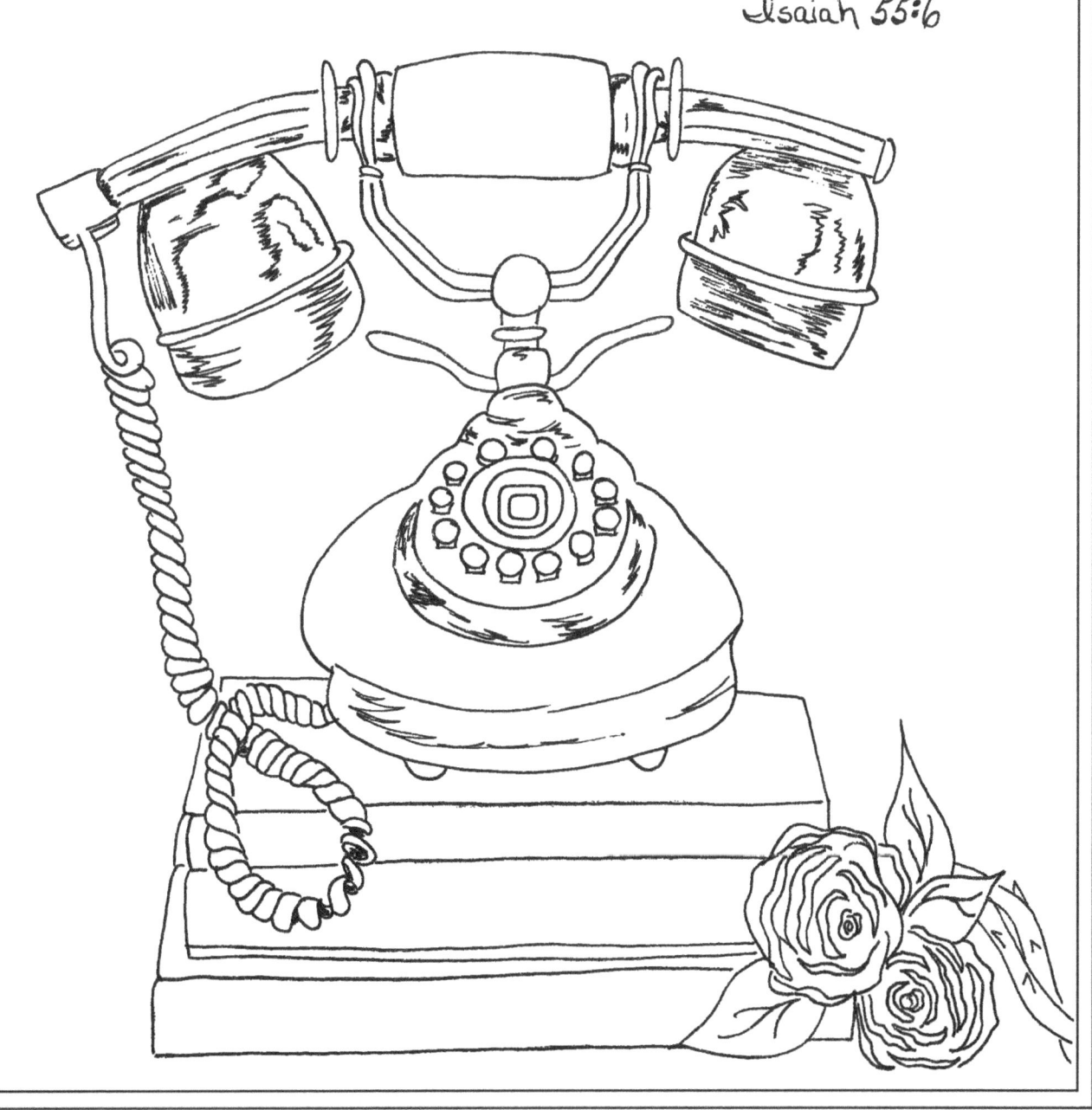

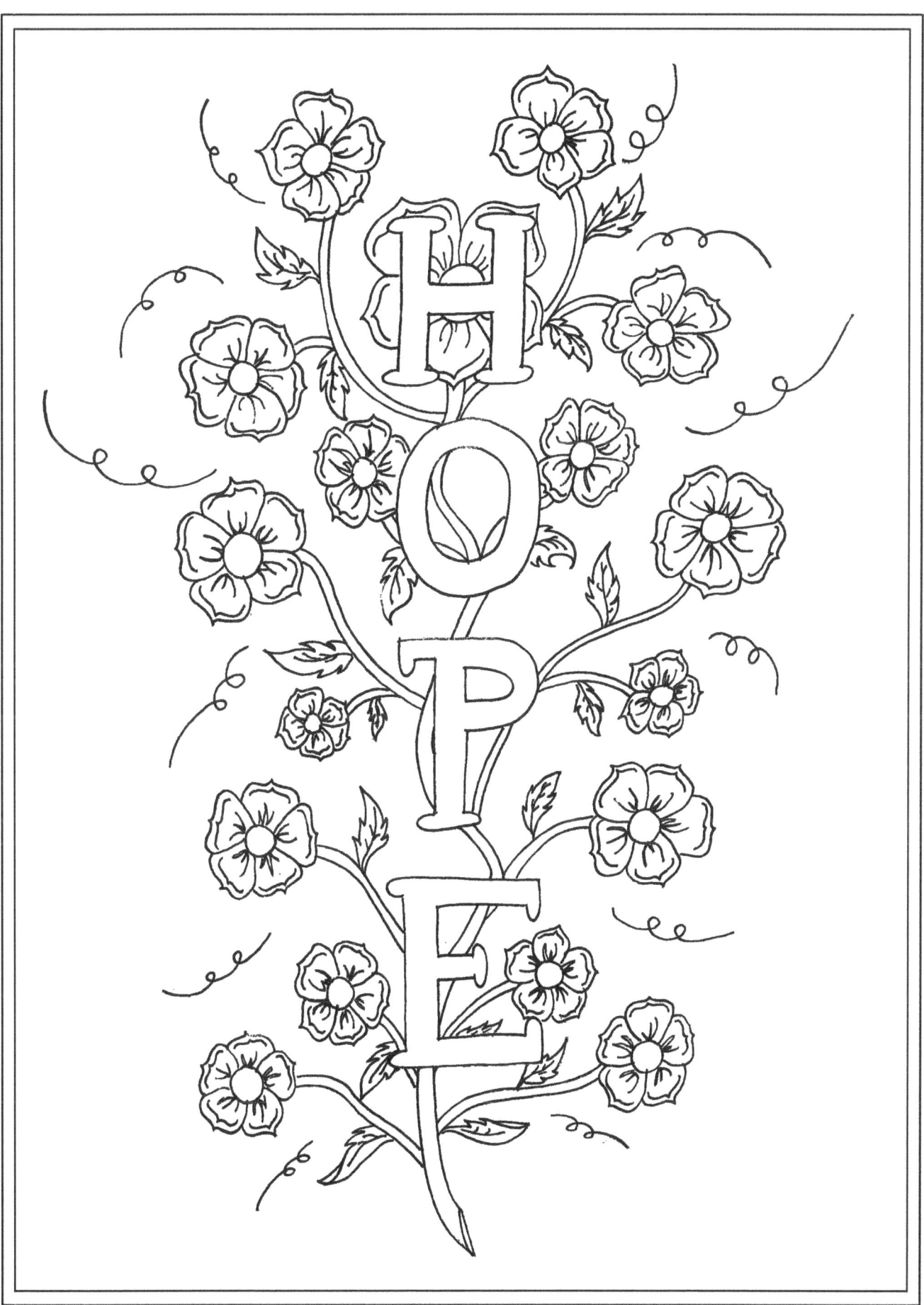

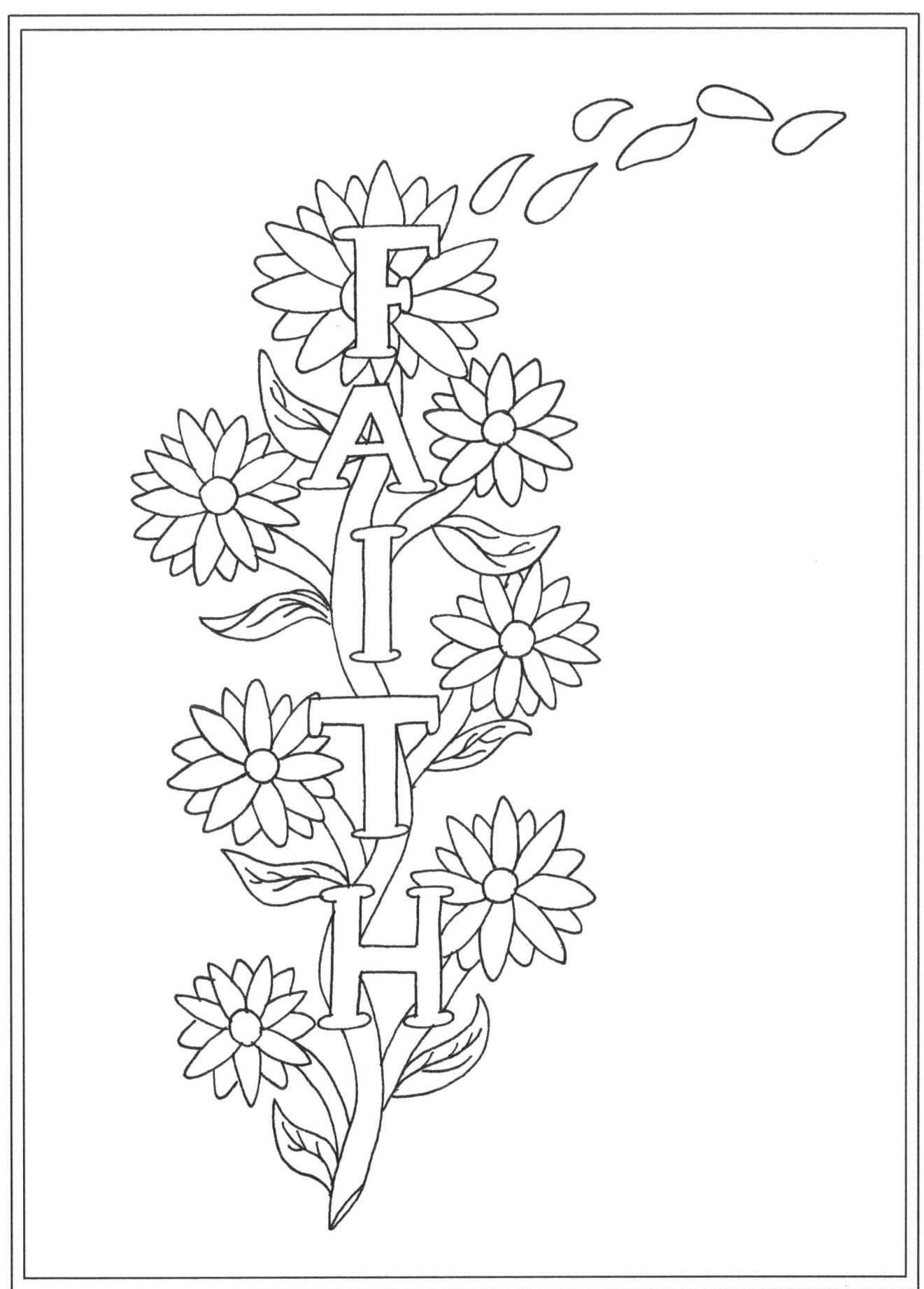

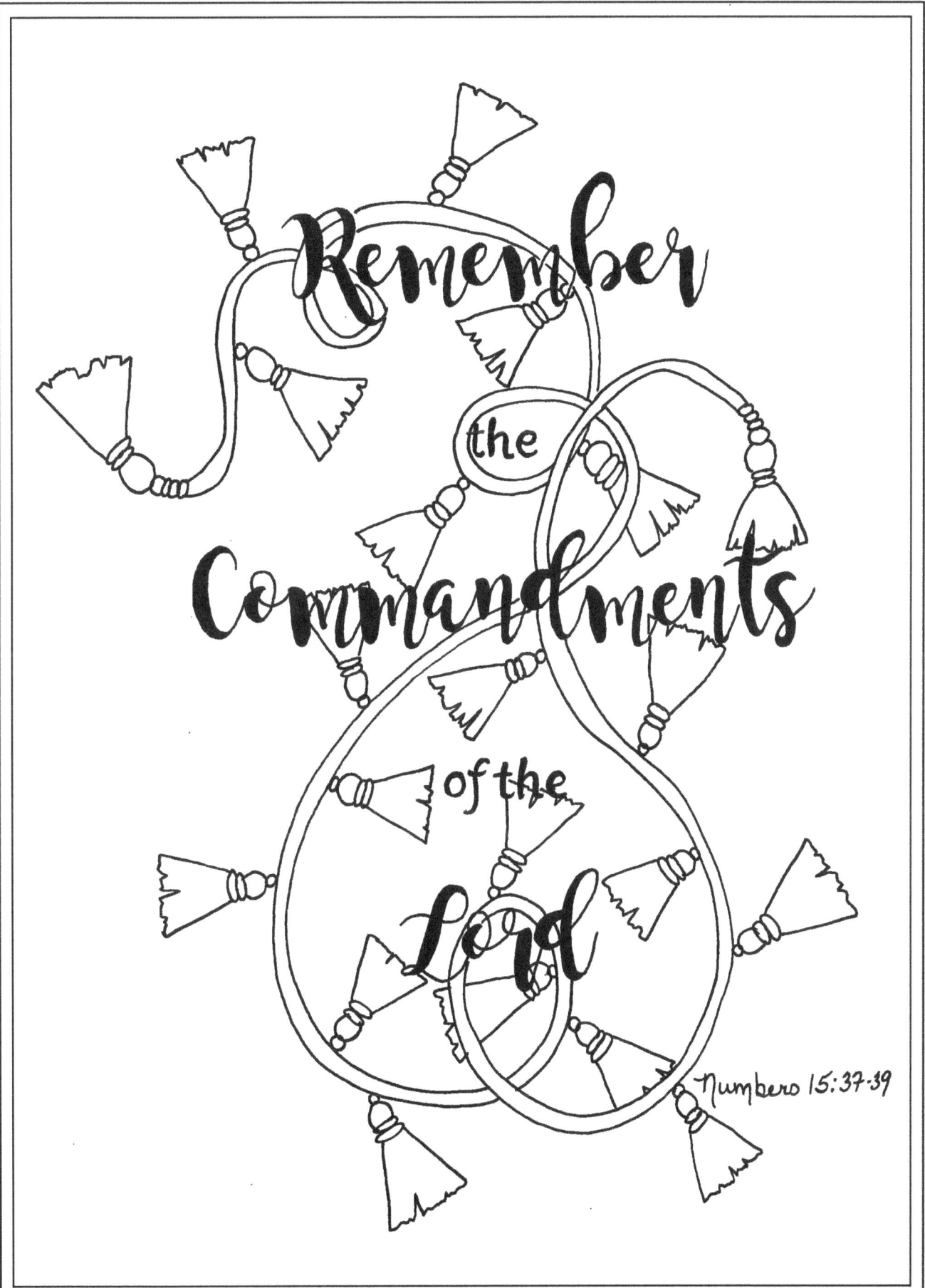

Remember the Commandments of the Lord

Numbers 15:37-39

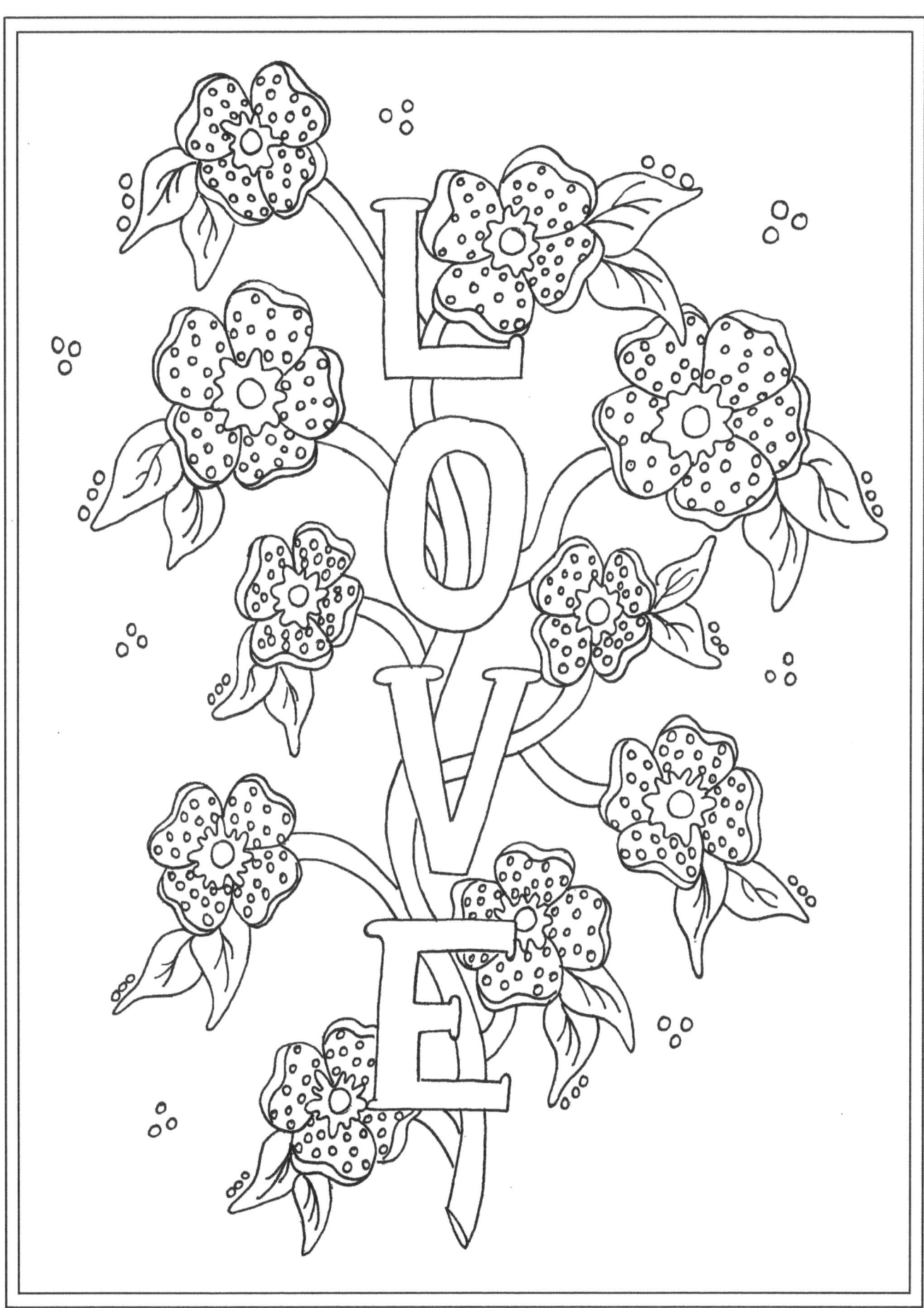

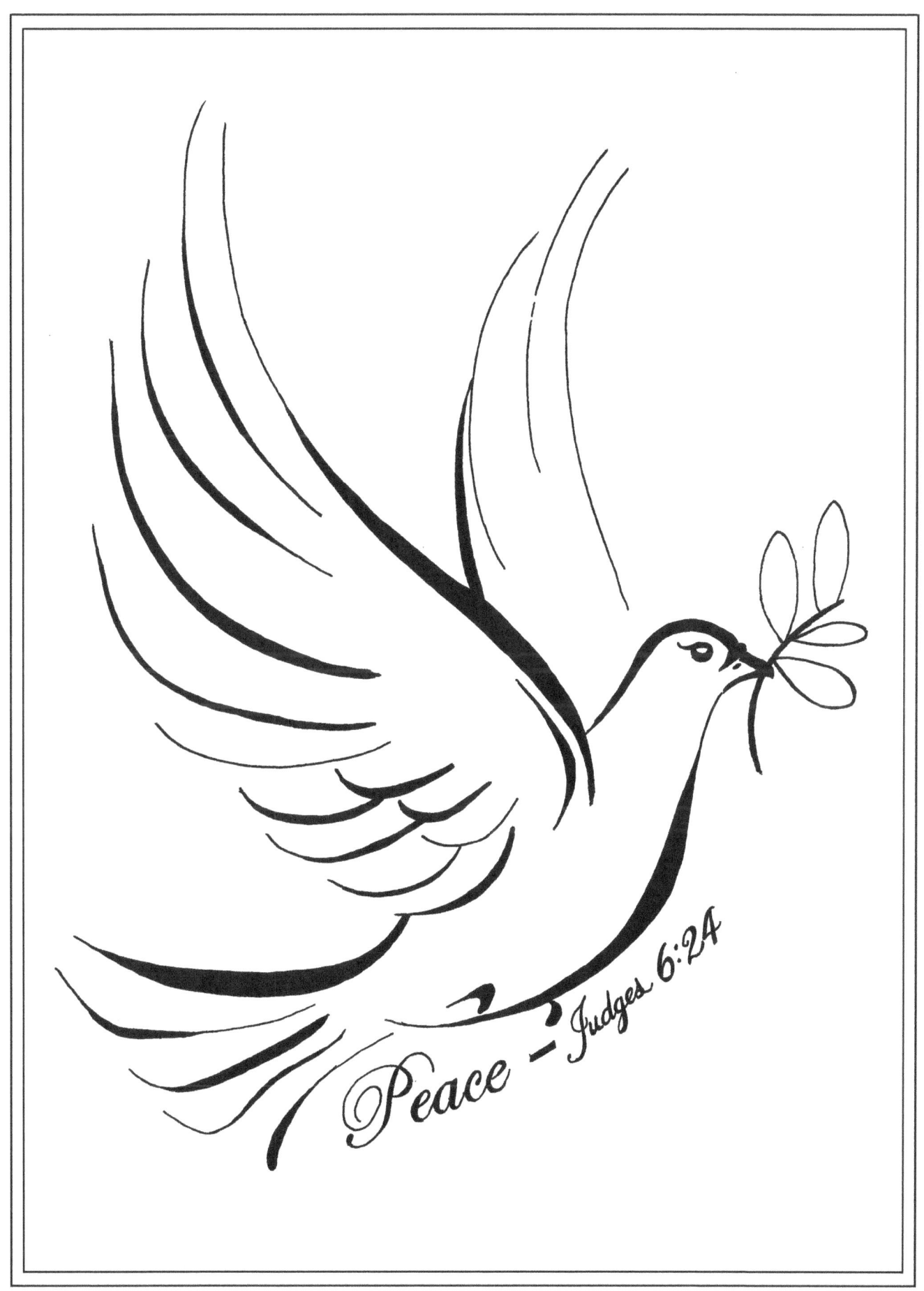

The Knowledge of

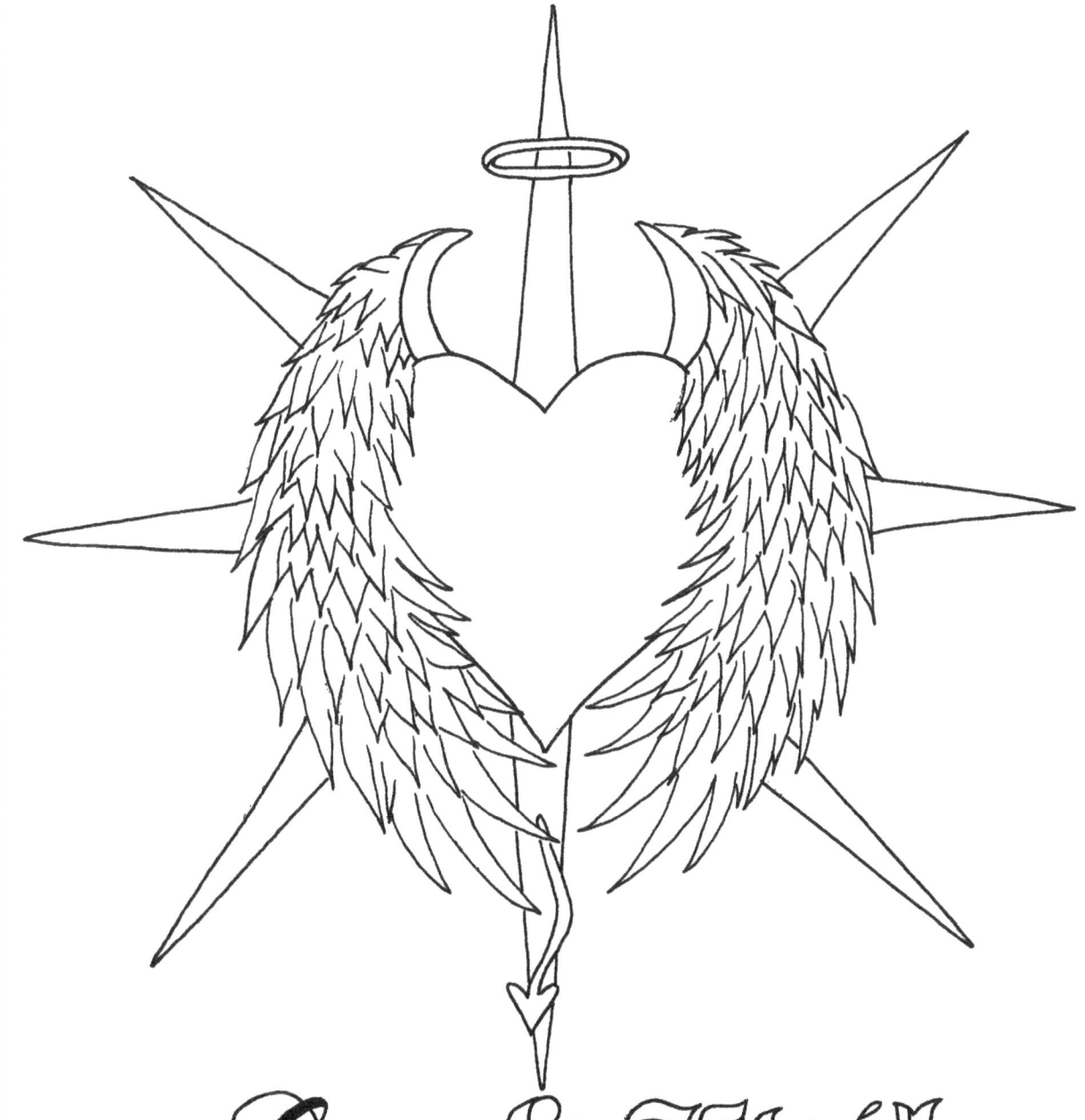

Good & Evil

Genesis 2:9

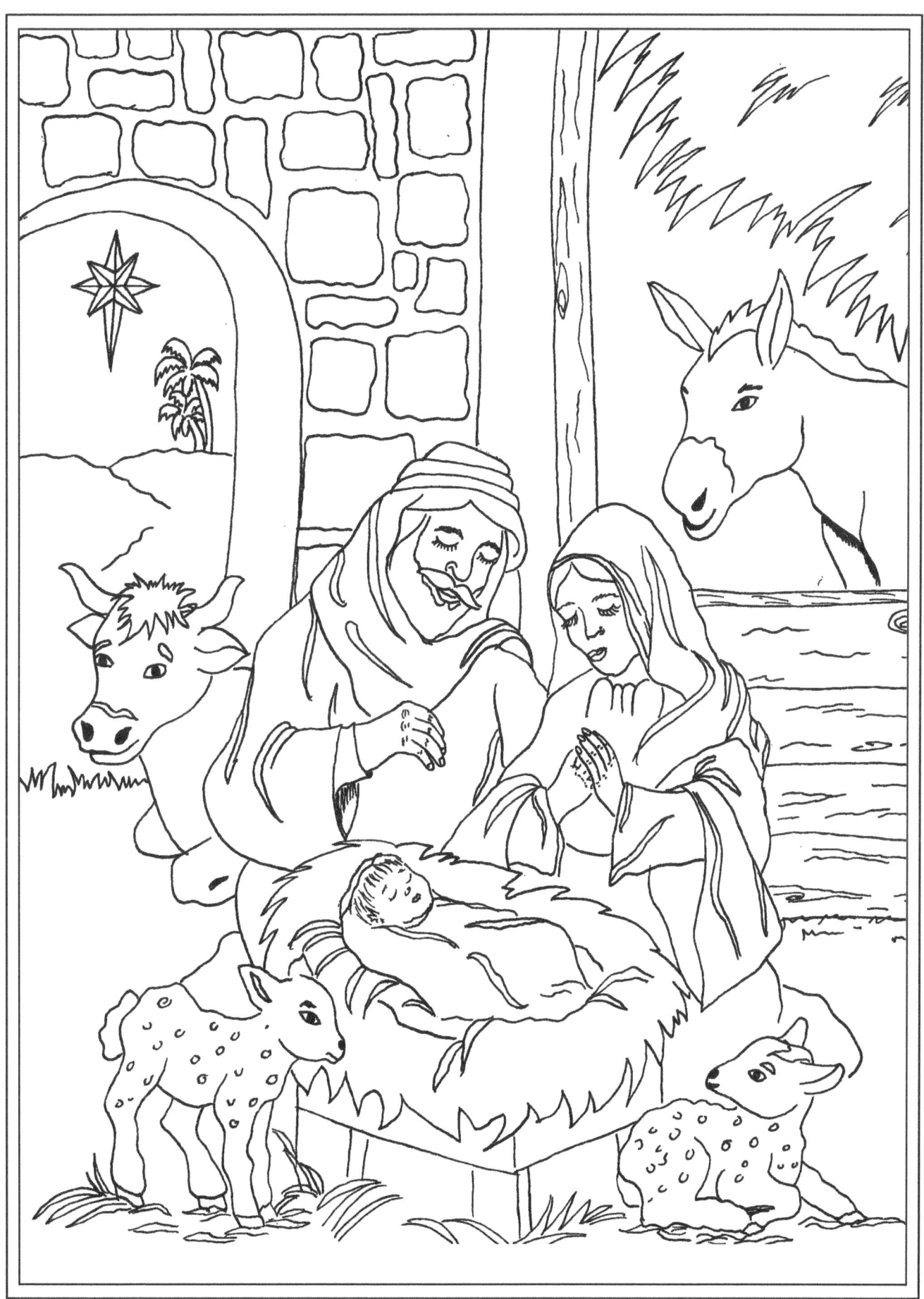

Whatever you do in **word** or **deed**,

do *everything* in the **name**

of the *Lord Jesus*

giving *thanks* to

God the **Father** through **Him**

1 Thessalonians 5:16-18

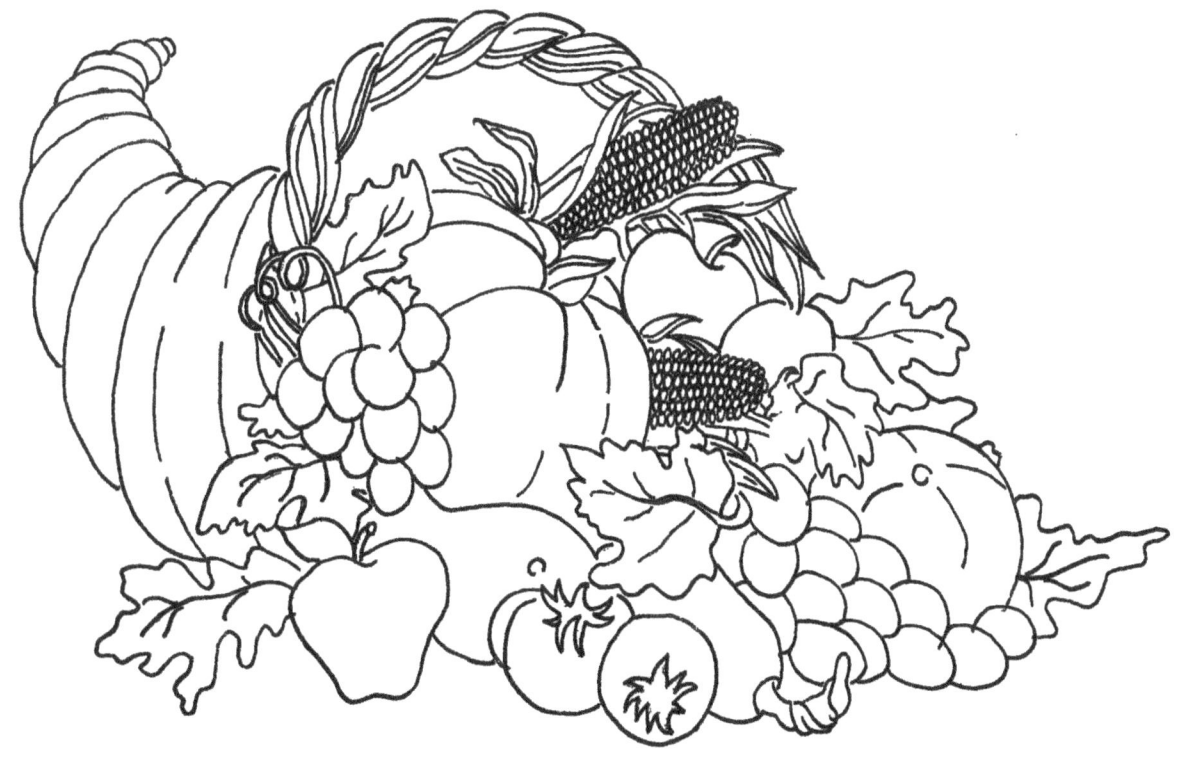

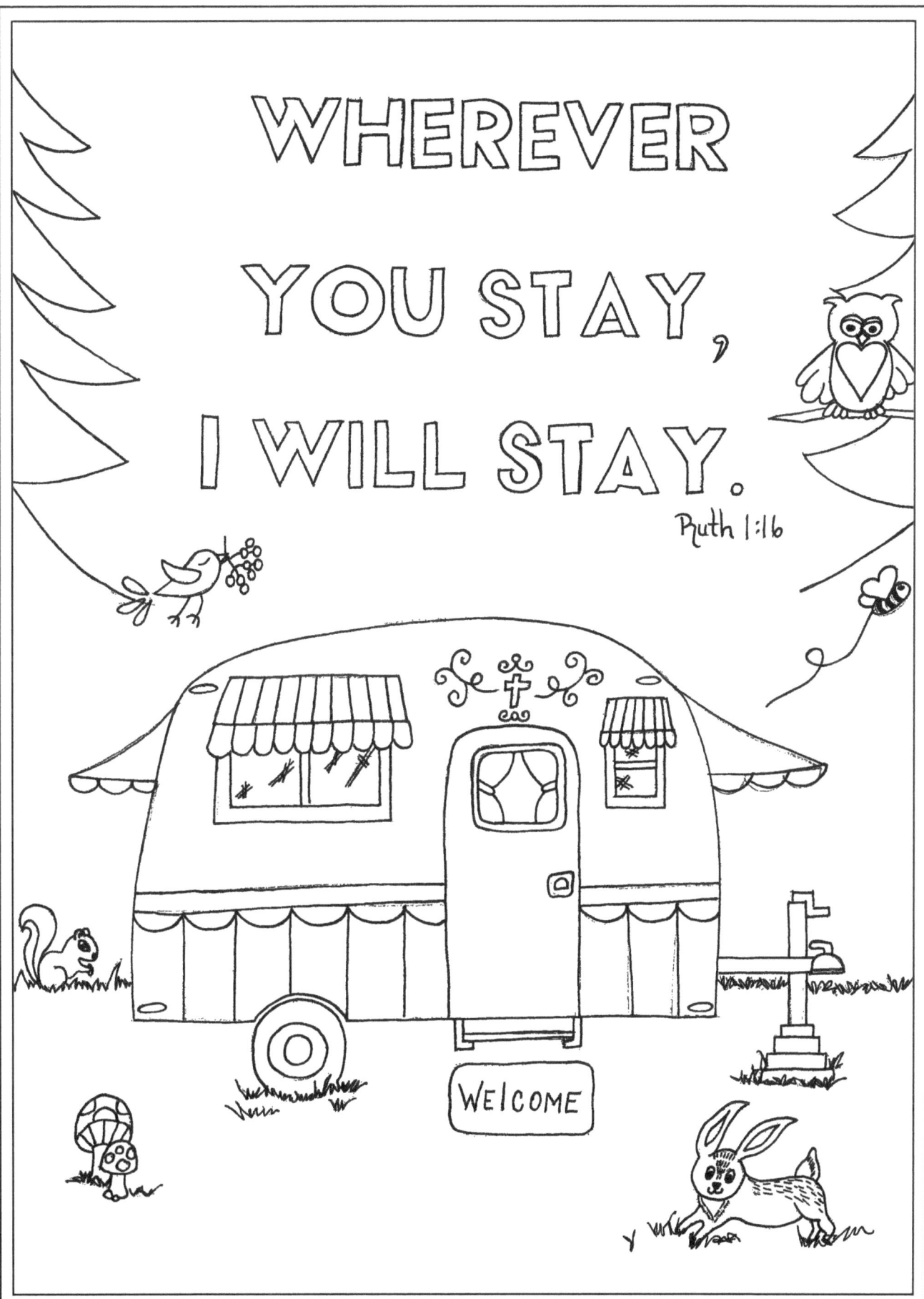

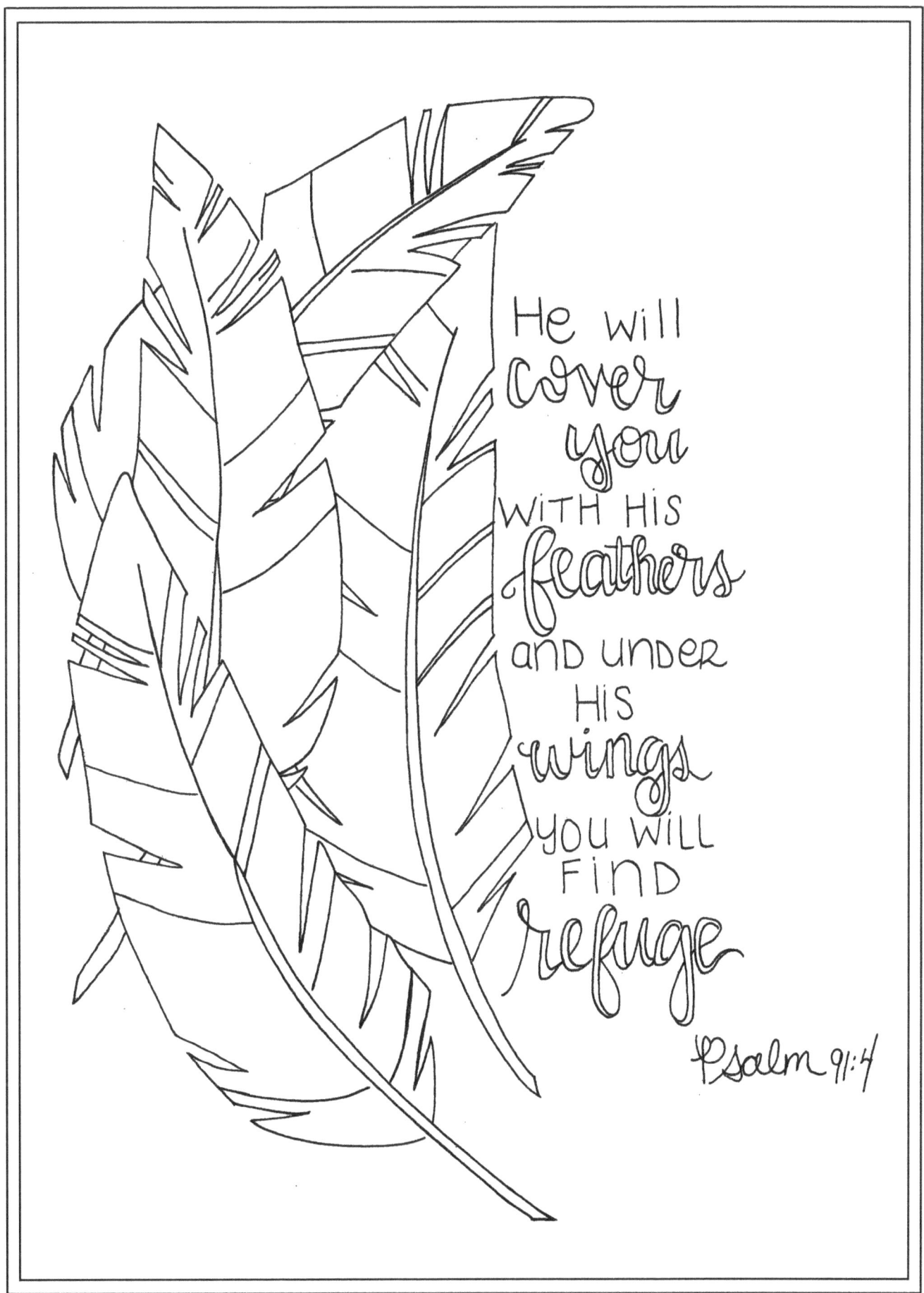

Keep watch because you do not know the day or the hour

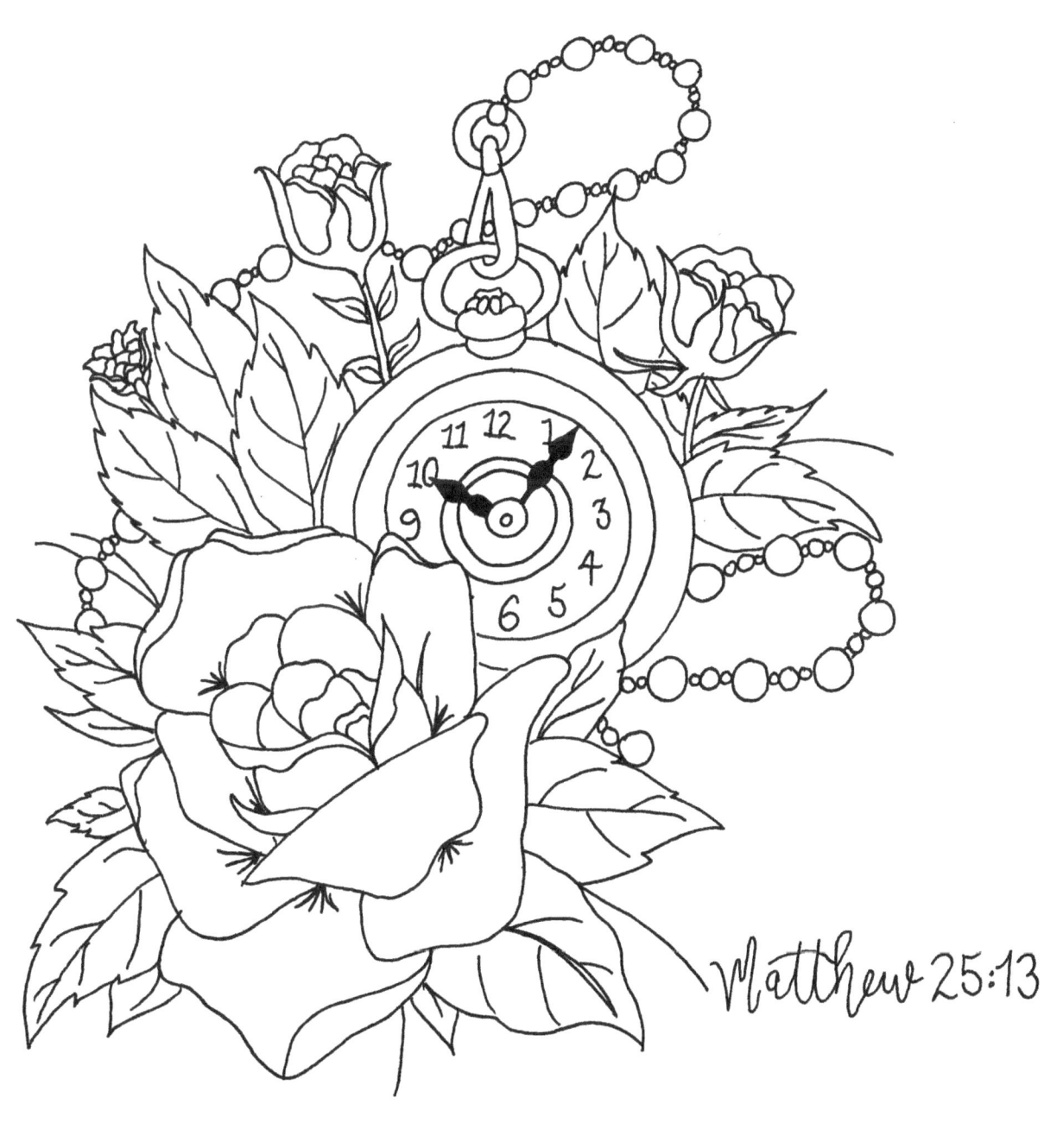

Matthew 25:13

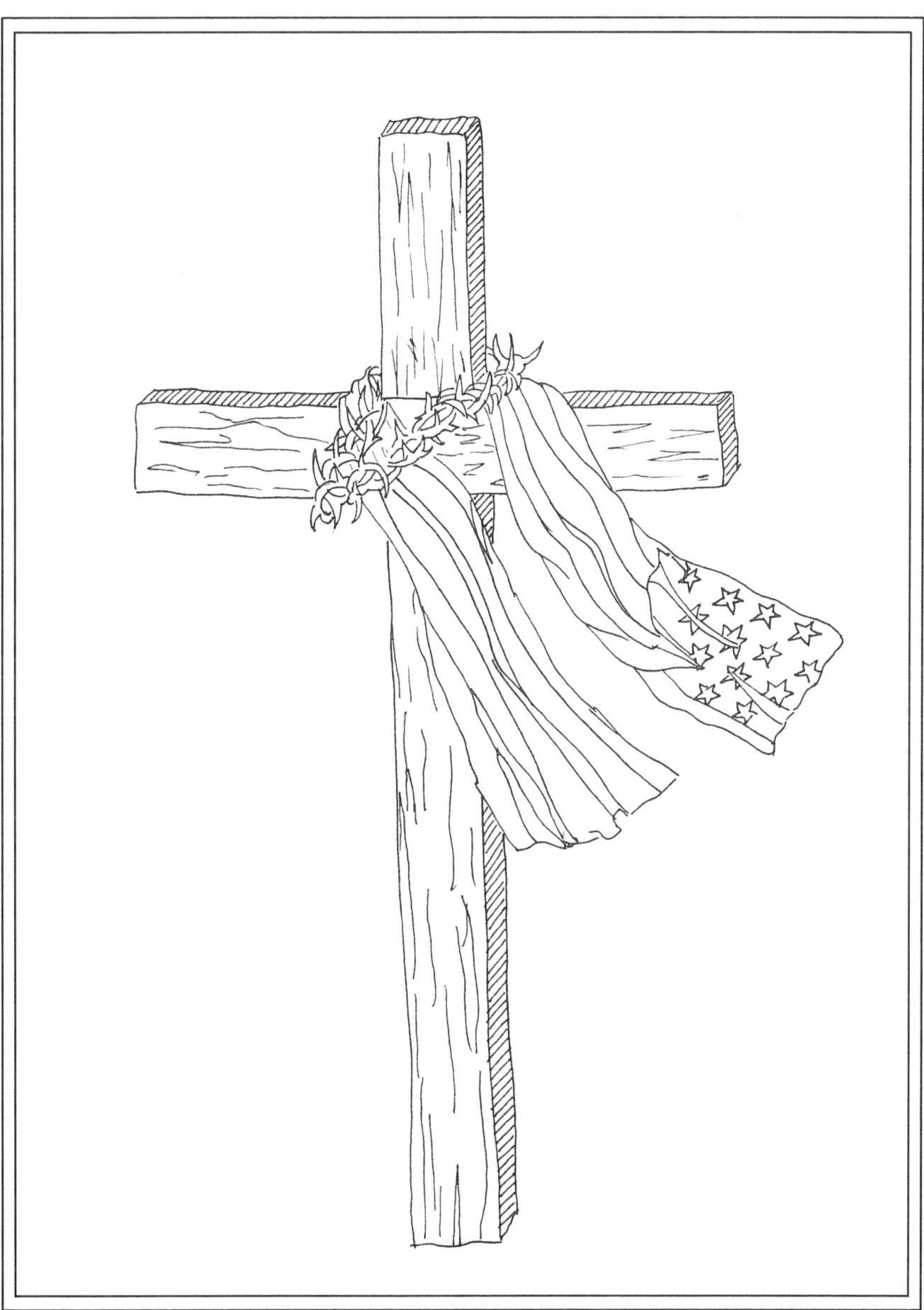

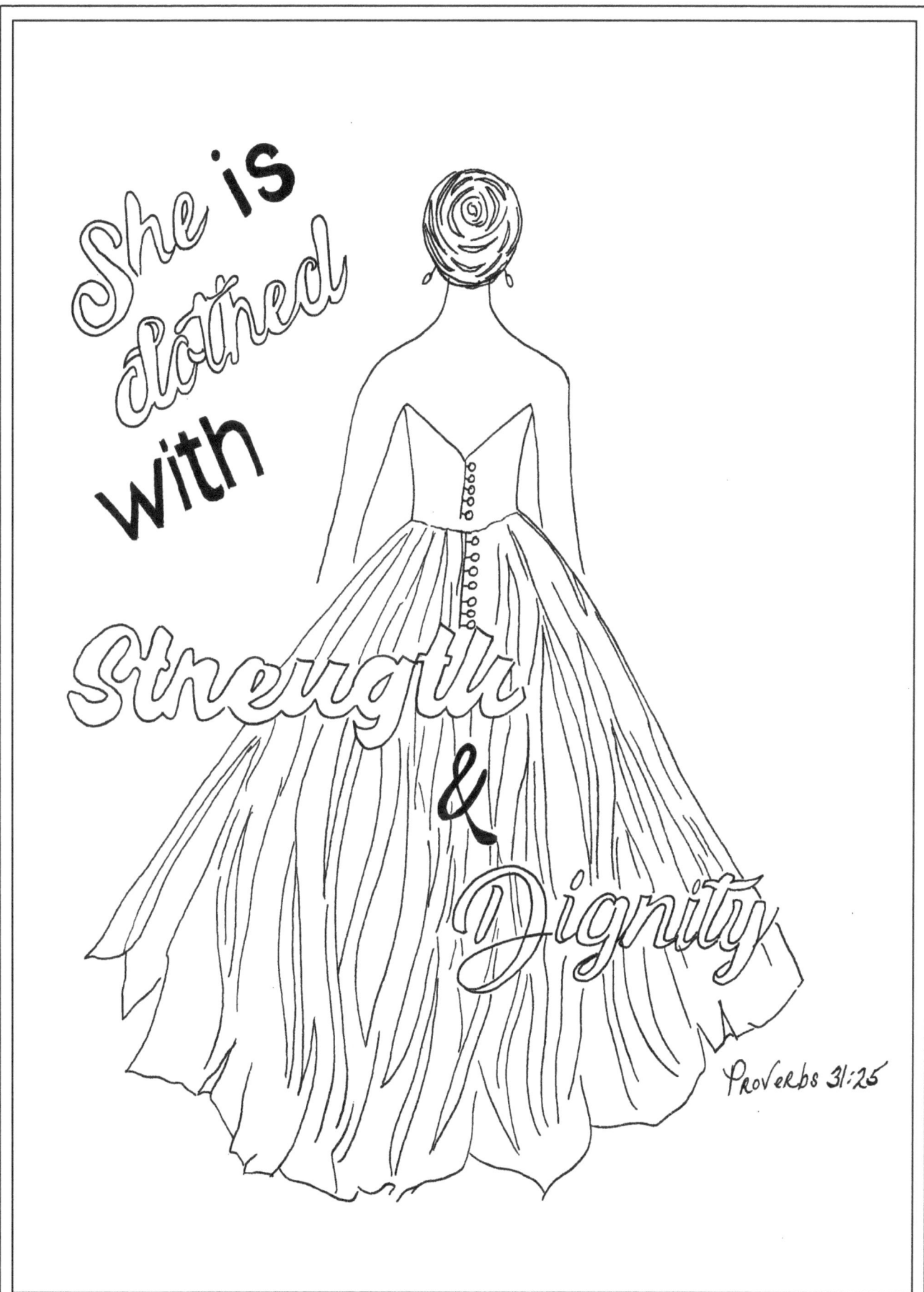

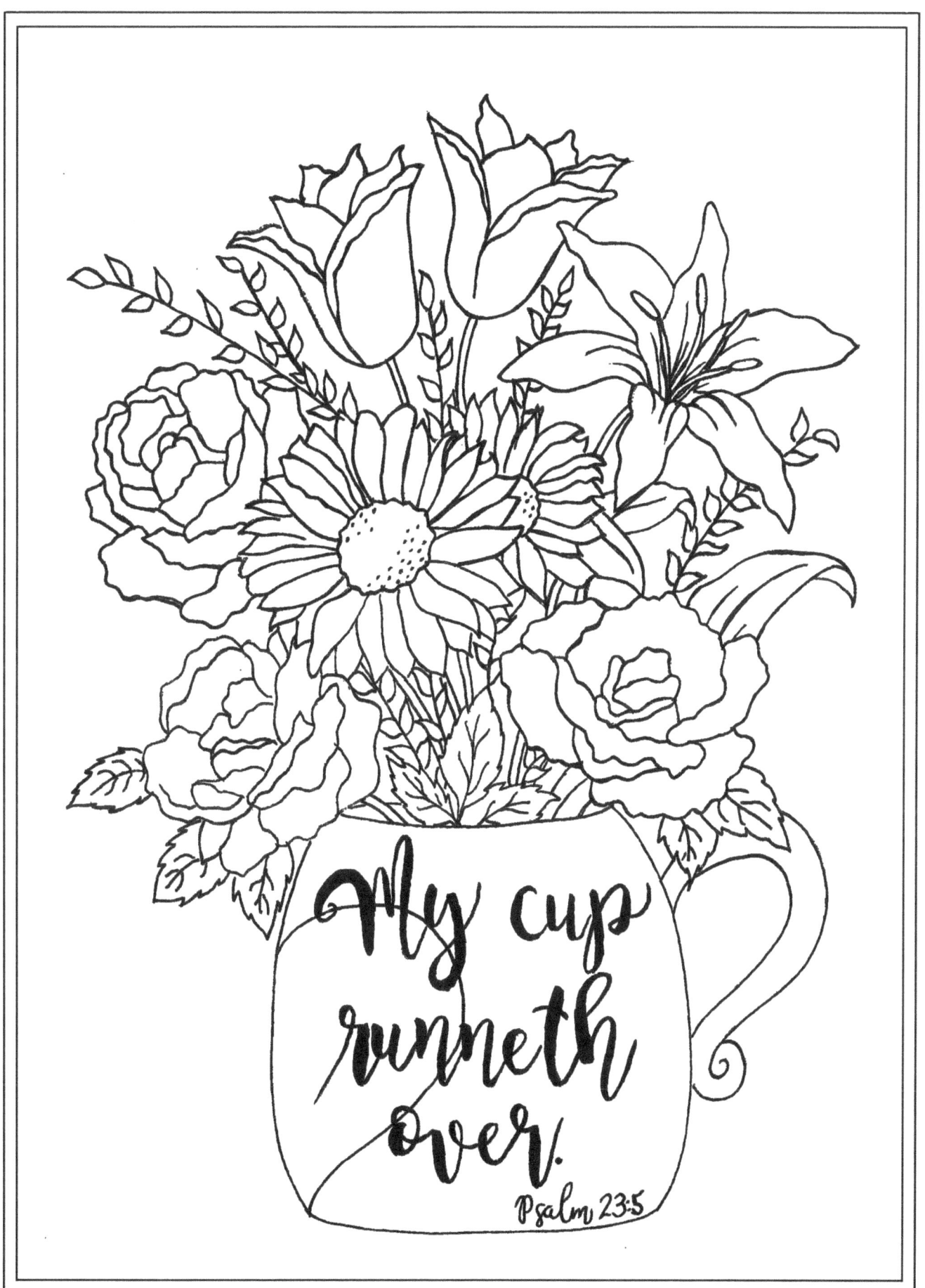

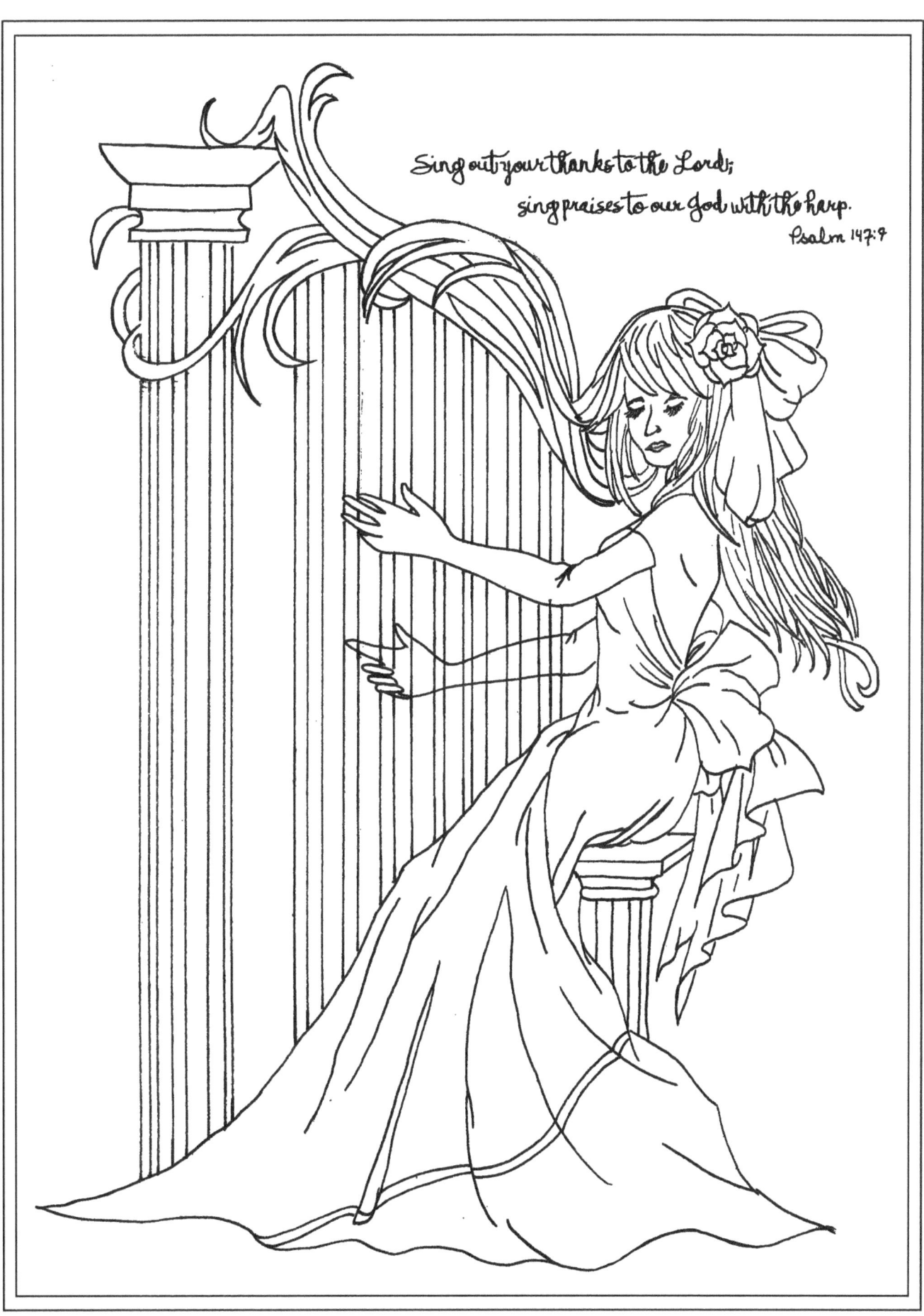

Sing out your thanks to the Lord;
   sing praises to our God with the harp.
                              Psalm 147:7

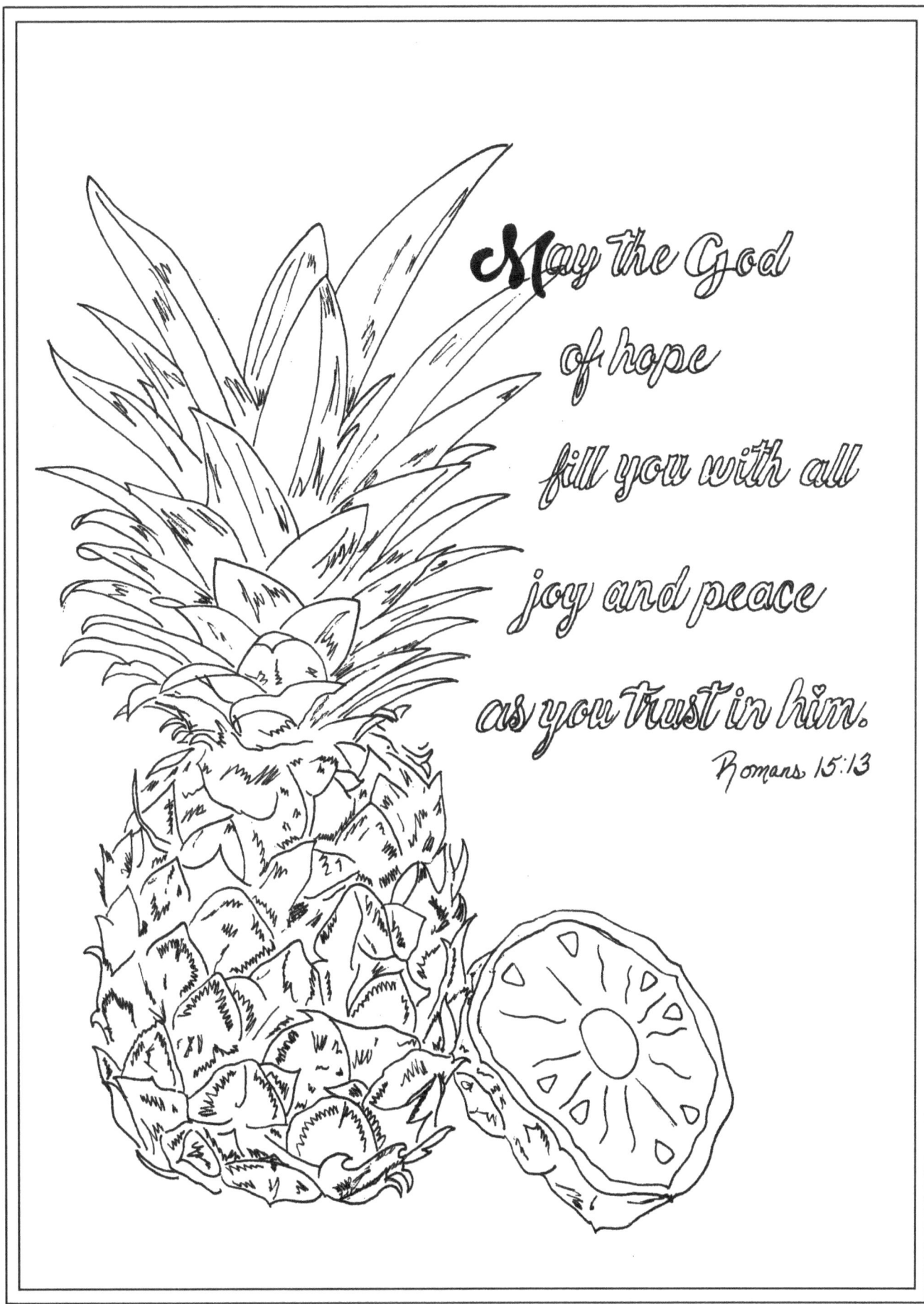

May the God
of hope
fill you with all
joy and peace
as you trust in him.
Romans 15:13

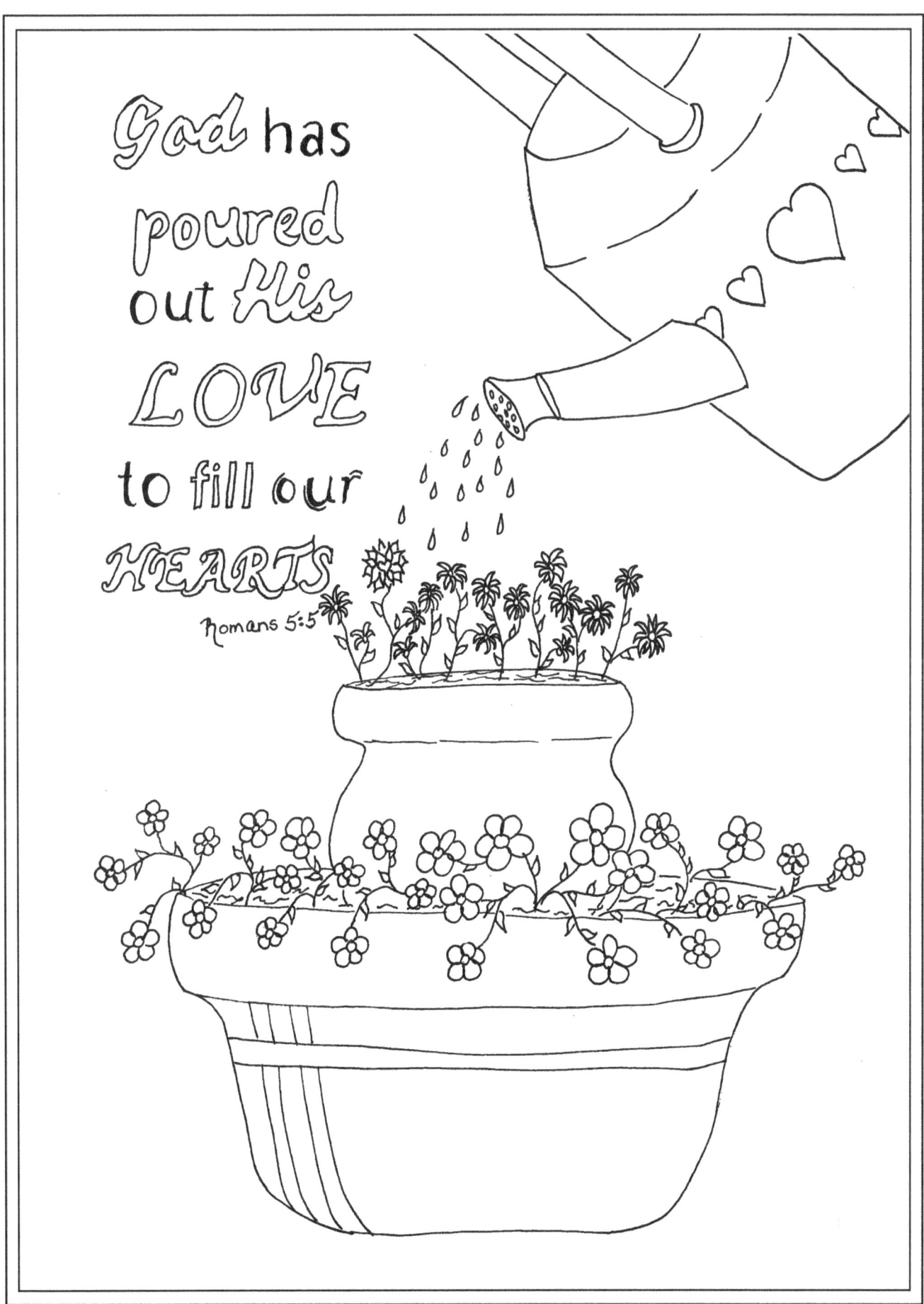

God has poured out *His* LOVE to fill our HEARTS

Romans 5:5

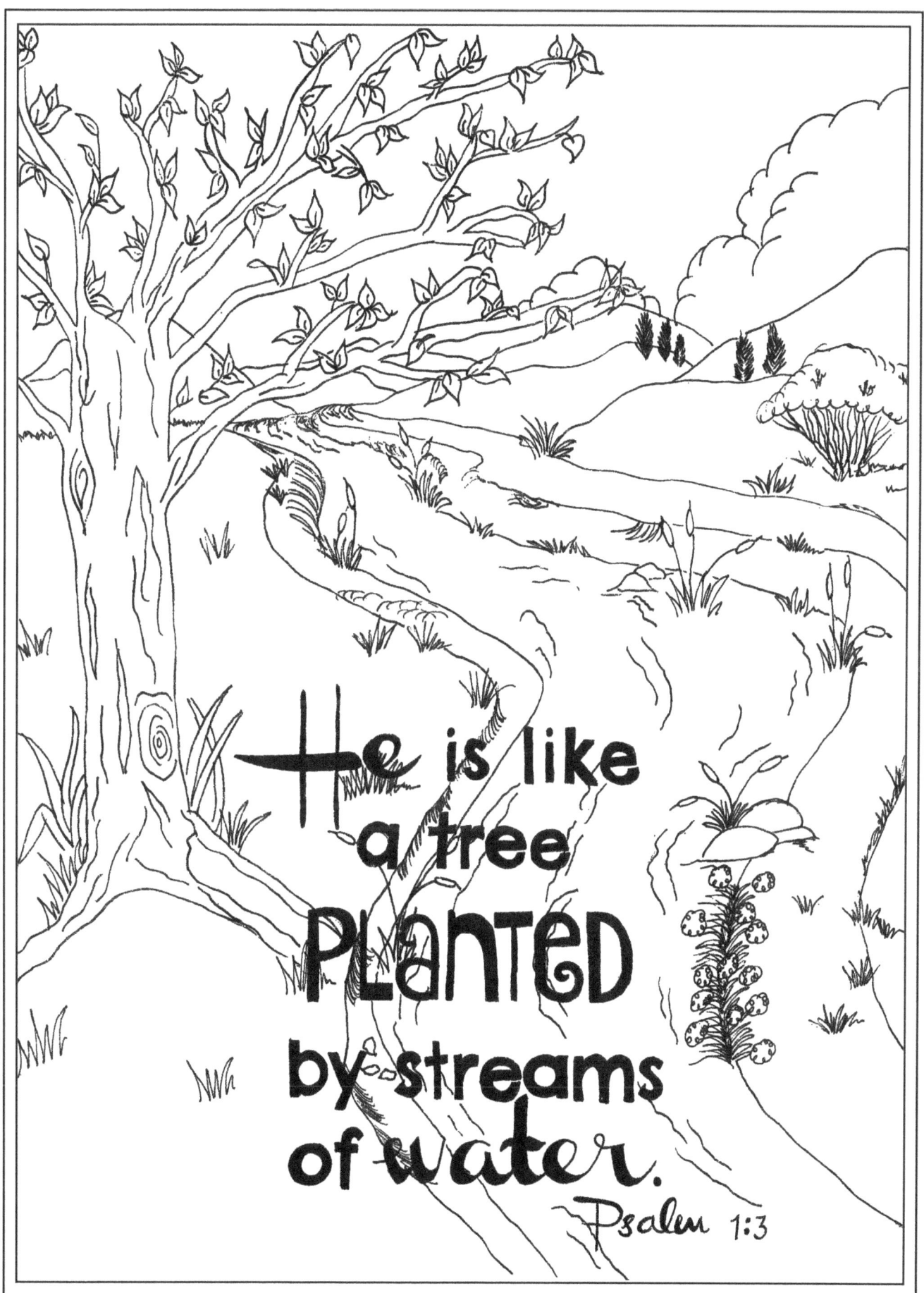

He is like a tree PLANTED by streams of water.

Psalm 1:3

www.ingramcontent.com/pod-product-compliance
Lightning Source LLC
Chambersburg PA
CBHW081250180526
45170CB00007B/2363